SOURCE PROBLEMS IN WORLD CIVILIZATION

CHINA'S CULTURAL TRADITION

What and Whither?

Derk Bodde

UNIVERSITY OF PENNSYLVANIA

HOLT, RINEHART AND WINSTON

New York — Chicago — San Francisco —
Toronto — London

June, 1966

PRINTED IN THE UNITED STATES OF AMERICA

PREFACE

The greatest problem in writing this book has been that of *space:* to compress more than three thousand years of Chinese cultural tradition into a little under one hundred pages, and at the same time give as balanced a presentation as possible to diverse topics and expressions of opinion. In view of the high degree of selectivity necessarily demanded by this task, I cannot flatter myself that the results will seem equally satisfactory to all. Some readers, for example, may possibly complain that the promise of the title is only partially realized by the treatment given to China's magnificent cultural achievements per se—her art, literature and the like—and that undue space has been allotted to matters of social psychology and political institutions. In reply I can only say that, whereas many writings have already helped to familiarize the public with China's art and literature, her distinctive sociological characteristics have not, in my opinion, commonly received the critical analysis they deserve in view of their crucial importance for an intelligent understanding of the Chinese scene, both past and present.

The same factor of space has also prevented me from quoting from original Chinese sources as frequently as I would like. I realize that what a modern scholar has to say about China may not always have the flavor and vividness of an ancient Chinese writing two thousand years ago. But whereas it is the modern scholar's task to explain, interpret, condense, and synthesize, the ancient Chinese rarely felt obligated in this way; moreover, he did not have to consider the needs and interests of the modern occidental reader. Persons, however, who wish to explore the original writings of Chinese literature and philosophy will find helpful bibliographies in many of the works cited in this book, notably those of Fung Yu-lan on philosophy (see footnotes 43 and 82) and that of James R. Hightower on literature (see footnote 77), as well as in our final "Bibliographical Note."

I am grateful to Mr. Laurence Sickman, Director of the William Rockhill Nelson Gallery of Art, Kansas City, for his great kindness in furnishing the reproduction of the beautiful painting from his museum which forms the second plate of this book, and to Mr. Reuben Goldberg, of the University of Pennsylvania Museum, for his similar kindness in making the excellent photographs which form the remaining plates.

DERK BODDE

Professor of Chinese
University of Pennsylvania
August, 1957

NOTE ON CHINESE NAMES

The names of Chinese persons are one of many causes for popular confusion regarding China. Traditionally, all such names follow a sequence exactly counter to our own; in other words, the surname or family name comes first, followed by a personal name (equivalent to what in the West would be called a "first" or "Christian" name). In the case of the contemporary philosopher *Fung* Yu-lan, for example, Fung is his surname (so that he is formally known to the world as Dr. or Professor Fung), whereas only friends and intimates would address him by his personal name, Yu-lan, used alone. Were this traditional practice consistently followed today, there would be relatively little trouble, but the situation is often complicated by modern Chinese who, in their associations with Westerners, bow to Western practice by placing their personal names first. Wing-tsit *Chan*, for example, is the name of Dartmouth's professor of Chinese history when talking to Americans, but among Chinese themselves he is known as *Chan* Wing-tsit.

Often a surname is distinguishable from a personal name through the fact that it is usually monosyllabic (Fung), whereas the personal name is frequently a disyllabic compound (Yu-lan). This by no means invariably follows, however, since many personal names as well as family names are monosyllabic (for example, *Hu* Shih, whose personal name is Shih). A few dissyllabic surnames, furthermore, also exist (such as *Kung-sun* or *Ssu-ma*); these, when they occur, are usually followed by a personal name which is monosyllabic (as in *Ssu-ma* Ch'ien), but sometimes by one consisting of two syllables (as in *Ssu-ma* Hsiang-ju).

Properly speaking, the two elements in a compound surname or personal name should always be hyphenated when romanized (as in *Ssu-ma* or Yu-lan). Some modern Chinese, however, prefer to transliterate their personal names as a single unhyphenated word (Lin Yutang, not Yu-tang), while others, in their associations with Westerners, drop their Chinese personal names entirely in favor of some Western equivalent (for example, Achilles Fang). A few reach a compromise by adopting a Western personal name, but at the same time following it with initials representing the two syllables of their original Chinese personal name (for example, Francis L. K. Hsu).

Though the Wade-Giles system of romanization has long been officially standard in the English-speaking world for transcribing Chinese names, it is not universally followed by all specialists, let alone the public at large. In the present book, therefore, names of modern Chinese writers are always cited according to the spellings personally favored by these writers, even when these spellings happen to diverge from the Wade-Giles system. (Hence the retention here of Fung Yu-lan, this being the form favored by Fung himself, even though in Wade-Giles it would be Feng Yu-lan.) For all other Chinese names and words, past and present, however, the Wade-Giles system has been followed. Only exceptions to this rule are the Jesuit-coined Latinizations Confucius and Mencius, long generally accepted as equivalents for Chinese originals which, in Wade-Giles, would appear as K'ung Tzu ("the Master K'ung") and Meng Tzu ("the Master Meng") respectively.

CONTENTS

PLATES

Following page 42

A. PROBLEMS OF THE TRADITION

1 The Problem of What, When, and Who

Culture: "The complex of distinctive attainments, beliefs, traditions, etc., constituting the background of a racial, religious, or social group."

Tradition: "Any belief, custom, way of life, etc., which has its roots in one's family or racial past; an inherited culture, attitude, or the like."

Literally followed, these very elastic definitions from *Webster's International Dictionary* would mean that the Chinese practice of sitting on high chairs (like ourselves but unlike most Asians), of eating with chopsticks, or of placing the guest of honor on the left (not the right) side could all be regarded as parts of China's cultural tradition. Obviously, we must here be more selective. In the following pages we shall try to confine ourselves only to those ideals and ideas, beliefs and attitudes, institutions and practices which, because of long duration, wide prevalence, and intrinsic importance, seem to be truly essential to any intelligent understanding of premodern China. At the same time we shall, when feasible, try to sketch their major changes in recent times.

At the outset we are confronted by several problems: first of all, the sheer bulk of Chinese history, for which continuous records exist covering well over three thousand years. Where, in this enormous time span, are we to find *the* most characteristic Chinese cultural tradition? For present purposes it will be convenient to divide Chinese history into three main periods:[1]

1. The pre-imperial age (ending 221 B.C.), also often known, because of its strong institutional similarities to medieval Europe, as China's age of feudalism. The China of this period consisted of many petty states grouped around the general area of the Yellow River valley in North China and ruled by hereditary noble houses commonly at war with one another. The state of Ch'in (from which our name China is probably derived) brought this period to an end by conquering the other states and amalgamating them into a new kind of centralized empire.

2. The imperial age (221 B.C. to the founding of the Republic in 1912), during which China expanded to her present geographical dimensions and was normally ruled as a single entity by a succession of major dynasties. Between these dynasties, however, occurred briefer transitional periods of disunity, warlordism, and civil war. The major feature of this age was its replacement of the former feudal nobility by a new ruling bureaucracy which was centrally appointed, nontitled, and theoretically nonhereditary. The members of this class (the "mandarins" of Western parlance) were highly educated men who shared the common ideology of Confucianism and, under many dynasties, were recruited for government service through the famous Chinese system of civil service examinations. Politically, the age is commonly known as that of the Confucian state; socially, because of

---

[1] These divisions, it should be stressed, are not universally accepted by all historians, some of whom apply to China the traditional European categories of ancient, medieval, and modern, whereas others describe all or most of prenineteenth-century Chinese history as "feudal," and still others apply yet different categories.

the dominance of the scholar-bureaucrats (who were often at the same time landlords), as that of Chinese "gentry" society.

3. The modern age (officially beginning in 1912, but actually going back to at least the early decades of the nineteenth century, when China was forcibly "opened" by the West). During this age the traditional Chinese way of life, as a monolithic entity, gradually crumbled under the impact of manifold pressures from the West, ideological as well as material. Fragments of the old system persisted, however, and continue today to influence the present scene powerfully at every point.

In this book we shall concern ourselves primarily with the cultural tradition which matured and assumed relatively fixed form during the imperial age (especially its last seven or eight centuries). In so doing, however, we shall always remember that some of its most important ideological ingredients—notably Confucianism and Taoism—go back to the preceding feudal age (especially its last three centuries). Of the three so-called "religions" of China, only Buddhism (which entered China from India in the first century A.D.) belongs wholly to the age of empire.

Other formidable problems for our inquiry are raised by questions like these: Who were the chief architects and perpetuators of China's cultural tradition? Were they solely those members of the politically dominant minority—probably never more than 10 or 15 per cent of the total population—who created China's literature, art, philosophy, and other major cultural achievements? Or did they also include the great mass of illiterate (and therefore usually inarticulate) physical workers—most of them peasants—whose continuous sweat and toil provided the economic basis of the whole structure? To what extent did the mores and thinking of the scholar in his study, or the official in his government office, coincide with those of the peasant in his rice paddy? Was the congruence sufficient to justify our speaking of *one* Chinese cultural tradition, or should we more properly speak of two: one for the literate few and another for the illiterate many?

Here, for lack of adequate indication to the contrary, we must follow the general assumption that, by and large, the cultural tradition of the upper class *did* dominate and permeate society as a whole to a very remarkable degree. In so doing, however, we must remember that we cannot always be really sure; it is unfortunately true that, before recent times, what we know about the peasant usually does not come from what he has himself said but from what members of the gentry have chosen to say for him. In some fields—notably cosmological speculation and religious attitudes—the differences between the two groups are very clear, and to these we shall try to call attention as they occur.

Even if we limit ourselves to sophisticated levels of thinking, moreover, it is easy to find ideas that are diametrically opposed to one another. Here, for example, is what two famous Confucianists, living within a few decades of each other, had to say on the topic of human nature:

> [The tendency of] human nature toward goodness is like the tendency of water to flow downward. Among men there are none who lack this [tendency toward] goodness, just as among waters there are none that do not flow downward.[2]

[2] Mencius (371?-289? B.C.), the second major figure in classical Confucianism. See *Mencius*, VIa, 2.

The nature of man is evil. His goodness is only acquired training.[3]

On spirits, ghosts, and immortality we are told (first and fourth to fifth centuries A.D.):

> People of the world say that the dead become ghosts, are conscious, and can hurt people. . . . [But] human death is like the extinction of fire. When a fire is extinguished, its light does not shine any more, and when a man dies, his intellect does not comprehend any more. . . . So if people nevertheless say that the dead have consciousness, they are mistaken.[4]

> The divinity of the hair is called "Deployed," the divinity of the two eyes is called "Abundant Light," the divinity of the top of the head is called "Father King of the East," . . . [and so on for other parts of the body]. . . . In the body of every man there are three Palaces, six Administrations, 120 Barriers, and 36,000 gods.[5]

Finally, on the question of whether or not China is morally and intellectually superior to the West (nineteenth century):

> As to human affairs, China emphasizes human relationships and honors benevolence and righteousness. In the West, on the contrary, a son does not take care of his father, a minister cheats his emperor, a wife is more honored than a husband.[6]

> We must first make ourselves respectable before we despise others. Now there is not a single one of the Chinese people's sentiments, customs, or political and legal institutions which can be favorably compared with those of the barbarians [i.e., the Westerners]. Is there any bit of Western culture which was influenced by China? Even if we beg to be on an equal footing with the barbarians, we still cannot achieve it, so how can we convert them to be Chinese?[7]

Obviously, clichés like "the oneness of the Orient" are dangerous when applied to China—let alone the rest of the Orient. Nonetheless, it is often possible for the specialist to distinguish the typical from the atypical in Chinese thought. He knows, for example, that though both Mencius and Hsün Tzu enjoyed great prestige in their own time, in the end it was Mencius' optimistic view of human nature that gained universal acceptance, whereas the pessimistic view of Hsün Tzu was decisively rejected. This book is written in the belief that, despite the shifting flow of ideas, institutions, and practices in Chinese history, it is possible to identify some of them, because of their persistence, homogeneity, and eventual triumph, as constituting *the* dominant Chinese cultural tradition.

[3] Hsün Tzu (*ca.* 298-*ca.* 238), the third major figure in classical Confucianism. See H. H. Dubs, trans., *The Works of Hsüntze* (London: Probsthain, 1928), p. 177.
[4] Wang Ch'ung (A.D. 27-*ca.* 100), an iconoclastic critic of popular beliefs. See Alfred Forke, trans., *Lun Heng: Philosophical Essays of Wang Ch'ung* (2 vols.; London: Luzac, 1907, 1911), I, 191, 196.
[5] A statement combined from two texts of religious Taoism (probably both fourth or fifth century A.D.), cited by Henri Maspero, *Le Taoisme* (Paris: Civilisations du Sud, 1950), p. 117.
[6] Statement by Yüan Tsu-chih (1827-1898), a writer, following his tour of Europe in 1883. See Ssu-yü Teng and John K. Fairbank, *China's Response to the West* (Cambridge, Mass.: Harvard University Press, 1954), p. 184.
[7] Statement by the noted reformer T'an Ssu-t'ung (1865-1898), cited by Teng and Fairbank, *op. cit.*, p. 160.

2 The Problem of Evaluation and Perspective

For at least two thousand years merchants, missionaries, diplomats, soldiers, adventurers, and others have been going to China—some by water, others over the long caravan route across Central Asia. Beginning in the ninth century, a few of them have left written records of what they saw—some brief, others bulky, some superficial, others profound. At first it was merchants of the Arab Empire who created the main bridge between East and West. Then in the thirteenth and fourteenth centuries, when the Mongols established their *pax tartarica* from the Danube to the China Sea, there arrived the first Europeans—not only the famous Marco Polo but also Christian missionaries of the Franciscan Order. In the sixteenth century the chief reporters were traders and adventurers from Portugal and Spain; in the seventeenth and eighteenth centuries they were the learned Jesuit missionaries, stationed in Peking; beginning in the nineteenth, the literature swelled, of course, to include men from all countries and all walks of life.

Much can be learned from these firsthand reports, if used properly, because, as the work of outsiders, they tell us things a Chinese himself would not bother or think about recording. On the one hand, they provide us with comparative standards for evaluating the East and West of their time; on the other, with historical perspectives for tracing the ebb and flow of Chinese civilization itself. Like most tourist literature, however, they often have serious limitations: superficiality, incompleteness, inaccuracy or bias, and the fact that few of their writers had scholarly preparation for recording an alien civilization. In not a few cases they seriously contradict one another.

Generally speaking, however, these travel accounts reveal one striking phenomenon: those prior to the nineteenth century are for the most part strongly favorable to China; those written later are not. Whether favorable or unfavorable, however, most of them make fascinating reading. The following is a small sampling from the large available literature.

One of the earliest accounts is an Arabic work of 851, traditionally, though perhaps wrongly, ascribed to a certain "Sulaiman the Merchant" who visited both China and India:[8]

> Whether poor or rich, young or adult, all Chinese learn to trace the characters and to write. . . When the cost of living increases, the government issues food from its reserves and sells it at less than the market price, so effectively that the high cost of living does not last long with them. . . . If a man is poor, he receives from the Treasury the cost for the remedy [of his illness]. . . . In each town there is a school and a school master for the instruction of the poor and their children; [these school masters] are supported at the expense of the Treasury. . . . China is more healthy [than India]. . . . One never sees a blindman, a cripple, or an infirm person there, whereas many of them are found in India.

Despite his omissions, inaccuracies, and superficialities, Marco Polo (in China 1275-1292) has left us an incomparably vivid account of the wealth, populousness, and grandeur of the China of his day:[9]

---

[8] See Jean Sauvaget, trans., *Ahbar as-Sin Wa l-Hind, Relation de la Chine et de l'Inde, rédigée en 851* (Paris: Société d'Edition "Les Belles Lettres," 1948), pp. 17-18, 21, 26.

[9] In Henry Yule and Henri Cordier, *The Book of Ser Marco Polo* (2 vols., 3rd ed.; London: Murray, 1921), I, 412-414; II, 185-190, 204.

You must know that the city of Cambaluc [modern Peking] hath such a multitude of houses, and such a vast population inside the walls and outside, that it seems quite past all possibility. . . . To this city also are brought articles of greater cost and rarity, and in greater abundance of all kinds, than to any other city in the world (I, 412-414).

The city [of Kinsay, modern Hangchow] is beyond dispute the finest and noblest in the world. . . . I repeat that everything appertaining to this city is on so vast a scale . . . that it is not easy even to put it into writing, and it seems past belief to one who merely hears it told. But I *will* write it down for you (II, 185-190).

The natives of the city [of Kinsay] are men of peaceful character. . . . They know nothing of handling arms, and keep none in their houses. You hear of no feuds or noisy quarrels or dissensions of any kind among them. Both in their commercial dealings and in their manufactures they are thoroughly honest and truthful, and there is such a degree of good will and neighbourly attachment among both men and women that you would take the people who live in the same street to be all one family (II, 204).

Polo's glowing account is in general corroborated by the slightly later Italian Franciscans, Friar Odoric of Pordenone (in China *ca.* 1323-1327) and Bishop Andrew of Perugia (who wrote from China in 1326). Thus Friar Odoric:[10]

Indeed in that country the number of people is so great that among us here it would be deemed incredible. . . . And no man ever seeketh alms, however poor he be, as long as he can do anything with his own hands to help himself. But those who are fallen into indigence and infirmity are well looked after and provided with necessaries. . . . And as for the women, they are the most beautiful in the world! (II, 178-179).

Likewise Bishop Andrew:

As to the wealth, splendour, and glory of this great emperor, the vastness of his dominion, the multitudes of people subject to him, the number and greatness of his cities, and the constitution of the empire, within which no man dares to draw a sword against his neighbour, I will say nothing, because it would be a long matter to write, and would seem incredible to those who heard it. Even I who am here in the country do hear things averred of it that I can scarcely believe (III, 72).

'Tis a fact that in this vast empire there are people of every nation under heaven, and of every sect, and all and sundry are allowed to live freely according to their creed. For they hold this opinion, or rather this erroneous view, that everyone can find salvation in his own religion. Howbeit we are at liberty to preach without let or hindrance (III, 74).

But of all travelers of the Mongol period, none, not even Marco Polo, can rival in scope the genial Arab Ibn Battutah, whose journeys carried him all the way from Spain and Central Africa as far as China, which he visited probably in 1347:[11]

This is a vast country; and it abounds in all sorts of good things, fruit, corn, gold and silver; no other country in the world can rival China in that respect.

[10] References for both Odoric and Andrew are to Henry Yule and Henri Cordier, *Cathay and the Way Thither* (4 vols., rev. ed.; London: Hakluyt Society, 1913-1916), II, 178-179; III, 72, 74.
[11] Yule and Cordier, *Cathay*, IV, 108, 114, 117-118.

> . . . The people of China of all mankind have the greatest skill and taste in the arts. This is a fact generally admitted. . . . As regards painting, indeed, no nation, whether of Christians or others, can come up to the Chinese; their talent for this art is something quite extraordinary. . . . China is the safest as well as the pleasantest of all the regions on the earth for the traveller. You may travel the whole nine months' journey to which the empire extends without the slightest cause for fear, even if you have treasure in your charge. . . . The harbour of Zayton [present Ch'üan-chou in South China] is one of the greatest in the world —I am wrong: it is *the* greatest!

Coming to the Portuguese and Spanish accounts of the sixteenth century, we select excerpts from Galeote Pereira, a Portuguese who was in south coastal China during 1549-1552, and whose favorable words are made all the more remarkable by the fact that he spent the greater part of these years in a Chinese prison:[12]

> By these means so uprightly things are ordered there, that it may be worthily accounted one of the best governed lands in all the world. . . . [I] think, that in all the world there be no better workmen for buildings, than the inhabitants of China (pp. 6, 8).

> Now will I speak of the manner the which the Chins do observe in doing justice, that it may be known how far these Gentiles do herein exceed Christians, that be more bounden than they to deal justly and in truth. . . . We poor strangers brought before them might say what we would, . . . yet did they bear with us so patiently, that they caused us to wonder, knowing specially how little any advocate or judge is wont in our country to bear with us. . . . We in a heathen country, . . . ignorant of that country's language, did in the end see our adversaries cast into prison for our sake, and deprived of their offices and honour for not doing justice (pp. 17, 20-21).

> There be hospitals in all their cities, always full of people; we never saw any poor body beg. . . . In this point of religion the Chins be at liberty, every one to worship and follow what liketh him best (pp. 30, 36).

The arrival in 1582 of the great Italian Jesuit Matteo Ricci (who died in Peking in 1610) marks a turning point in Sino-Western cultural relations. He is the first European to acquire a real mastery of Chinese learning, and his lengthy diary (posthumously edited and published in Latin in 1615 by another Jesuit, Nicolas Trigault) provided the West with an incomparably more detailed and accurate picture of China than any previously available. From this remarkable book we can quote only a few excerpts:[13]

> Due to the great extent of this country . . . , it can be safely asserted that nowhere else in the world is found such a variety of plant and animal life. . . . Everything which the people need for their well-being and sustenance, whether it be for food or clothing or even delicacies and superfluities, is abundantly produced within the borders of the kingdom and not imported from foreign climes (p. 10).

[12] C. R. Boxer, ed., *South China in the Sixteenth Century* (London: Hakluyt Society, 1953), pp. 6, 8, 17, 20-21, 30, 36.
[13] Matthew Ricci, trans. Louis J. Gallagher, *China in the Sixteenth Century: The Journals of Matthew Ricci: 1583-1610* (New York: Random House, 1953), pp. 10, 54-59, 93-97.

It seems to be quite remarkable when we stop to consider it, that in a kingdom of almost limitless expanse and innumerable population, and abounding in copious supplies of every description, . . . neither the King nor his people ever think of waging a war of aggression. They are quite content with what they have and are not ambitious of conquest. . . . Another remarkable fact, and quite worthy of note as marking a difference from the West, is that the entire kingdom is administered by the Order of the Learned, commonly known as The Philosophers [the Confucian scholar-officials]. The responsibility for orderly management of the entire realm is wholly and completely committed to their charge and care. . . .

The order and harmony that prevails among magistrates, both high and low, . . . is also worthy of admiration. . . . Every third year . . . a rigorous investigation is made concerning the magistrates of every province in the entire kingdom. . . . The purpose of this investigation is to determine who shall be retained in public office, how many are to be removed, and the number to be promoted or demoted and punished, if need be. There is no respect for persons in this searching inquisition. I myself have observed that not even the King would dare to change a decision settled upon by the judges of this public investigation. . . . It is a general law that no judge may hold court in the province in which he was born. . . . This is a precaution against favoring relatives and friends. . . . No one is permitted to carry arms within city limits, not even soldiers or officers. . . . Fighting and violence among the people are practically unheard of. . . . On the contrary, one who will not fight and restrains himself from returning a blow is praised for his prudence and bravery (pp. 54-59).

Of all the pagan sects known to Europe, I know of no people who fell into fewer errors in the early ages of their antiquity than did the Chinese. . . . The books of rare wisdom of their ancient philosophers . . . are still extant and are filled with most salutary advice on training men to be virtuous. In this particular respect, they seem to be quite the equals of our own most distinguished philosophers. . . . The ultimate purpose and the general intention of this sect, the [Confucian] literati, is public peace and order in the kingdom. They likewise look toward the economic security of the family and the virtuous training of the individual. The precepts they formulate are certainly directive to such ends and quite in conformity with the light of conscience and with Christian truth. . . . Their writings explain at length the second precept of charity: "Do not do unto others what you would not wish others to do unto you." It really is remarkable how highly they esteem the respect and obedience of children toward parents, the fidelity of servants to a master, and devotion of the young to their elders (pp. 93, 97).

We have no space here to dwell upon the flood of similarly laudatory accounts which poured from the Jesuits in Peking during the seventeenth and eighteenth centuries. It need only be remarked that they left a profound impression on some of the greatest Europeans of their day, notably Voltaire, who in 1764 wrote in his *Dictionnaire philosophique:* "One need not be obsessed with the merits of the Chinese to recognize that the organization of their empire is in truth the best that the world has ever seen." [14]

Yet when we come to the nineteenth century, we find that amazing reversal of opinion to which we have already referred. From the enormous literature of the period only two striking examples can be given here. The first is the English

[14] Voltaire, *Oeuvres complètes* (Gotha ed. of 1785), XXXVIII, 492; cited in Adolph Reichwein, *China and Europe: Intellectual and Artistic Contacts in the Eighteenth Century* (London: Kegan Paul, 1925), p. 89.

Protestant missionary Arthur H. Smith, who writes as follows in his widely read book, *Chinese Characteristics:*[15]

> Hopeless poverty is the most prominent fact of the Chinese Empire (p. 195).

> There can be no doubt in the mind of anyone who knows the Chinese that they display an indifference to the sufferings of others which is probably not to be matched in any other civilized country (p. 213).

> The ordinary speech of the Chinese is so full of insincerity . . . that it is very difficult to learn the truth in almost every case. In China it is literally true that a fact is the hardest thing in the world to get (p. 271).

> Chinese society resembles some of the scenery in China. At a little distance it appears fair and attractive. Upon a nearer approach, however, there is invariably much that is shabby and repulsive, and the air is full of odours which are not fragrant (p. 318).

> What China needs is righteousness, and in order to attain it, it is absolutely necessary that she have a knowledge of God and a new conception of man, as well as of the relation of man to God. She needs a new life in every individual soul, in the family, and in society. The manifold needs of China we find, then, to be a single imperative need. It will be met permanently, completely, only by Christian civilization (p. 330).

With even greater bitterness the American Protestant missionary S. Wells Williams writes in his famous compendium, *The Middle Kingdom:*[16]

> They are vile and polluted in a shocking degree; their conversation is full of filthy expressions and their lives of impure acts. . . . More uneradicable than the sins of the flesh is the falsity of the Chinese, and its attendant sin of base ingratitude; their disregard of truth has perhaps done more to lower their character than any other fault. . . . Thieving is exceedingly common, and the illegal exactions of the rulers . . . are most burdensome. . . . Hospitality is not a trait of their character; on the contrary, the number and wretched condition of the beggars show that public and private charity is almost extinct. . . . The politeness which they exhibit seldom has its motive in good-will, and consequently, when the varnish is off, the rudeness, brutality, and coarseness of the material is seen. . . . Female infanticide . . . ; . . . the alarming extent of the use of opium . . . ; the universal practice of lying and dishonest dealings; the unblushing lewdness of old and young; harsh cruelty toward prisoners . . . —all form a full unchecked torrent of human depravity, and prove the existence of a kind and degree of moral degradation of which an excessive statement can scarcely be made, or an adequate conception hardly be formed.

In contrast to these somber views, it is possible to find a very few nineteenth-century writers who perpetuate the earlier favorable picture. One of the most striking is the French agricultural expert and diplomat Eugène Simon:[17]

> I can state that in Hankow, a town in which I lived for some time, only one murder took place in thirty-four years (p. 7). Their very appearance shows that

---

[15] Arthur H. Smith, *Chinese Characteristics* (New York: Revell, 1894), pp. 195, 213, 271, 318, 330.

[16] S. Wells Williams, *The Middle Kingdom* (1882 ed., rev.; New York: Scribner's, 1907), I, 834-836. First published in 1848.

[17] Eugène Simon, *China: Its Social, Political and Religious Life* (London: Marsten, Searle & Rivington, 1887), pp. 7, 8, 22, 23. Eng. trans. of his *La cité chinoise* (Paris, 1885).

there exists between rich and poor, or rather the less well-to-do . . . much less distance and difference than among ourselves (p. 8). Speaking as one who passed ten years in China, and travelled throughout the country from north to south, and east to west, I can declare that I have never known a case of infanticide (p. 22). Nowhere do there exist so few beggars as in China (p. 23).

Among prenineteenth-century writings, likewise, it is occasionally possible to find critical as well as favorable passages. This is true, for example, of the Ricci-Trigault journals (a fact which strengthens our confidence in their honesty):[18]

> Many of them, not being able to forgo the company of women, sell themselves to wealthy patrons, so as to find a wife among his women servants. . . . The result of this practice is that the whole country is virtually filled with slaves. . . . A far more serious evil here is the practice in some provinces of disposing of female infants by drowning them. . . . The penal laws of the country do not seem to be too severe, but it seems that as many are illegally put to death by the magistrates as are legally executed. This is brought about by a fixed and ancient custom of the country permitting a magistrate, without any legal process or judgment, to subject a person to flogging whom it might please him to do so. . . . So great is the lust for domination on the part of the magistrates that scarcely anyone can be said to possess his belongings in security, and everyone lives in continual fear of being deprived of what he has, by a false accusation.

Passages such as these and those of Simon are nevertheless rare for their respective periods. How, then, to explain the extraordinary change in attitude? Possible reasons are suggested by the following questions:

1. To what extent do the tremendous economic and social changes experienced by the West during the nineteenth century explain its shift in attitude to China, a country where comparable changes did not occur? (It is worth noting, for example, that in England the death penalty for stealing five shillings was not abolished until 1818, and then only after four Parliamentary rejections. In eighteenth-century China, on the other hand, capital punishment was not applied to theft save for a third repetition, amounting to fifty ounces or more of silver.)

2. To what extent did the new attitude reflect the growing disintegration of the old way of life in China itself, occurring at the very time the West was forging ahead? (It seems not improbable that internal dynastic decline, political disorders, disruption of the native economy by Western inroads, and population pressure had by the 1930's all combined to bring the economic position of the peasant to a point actually below what it had been one or two centuries earlier.)

3. To what extent was it a Western reaction to nineteenth-century Chinese antiforeignism—itself a reaction to repeated humiliations suffered by China from the West?

4. To what extent did it reflect the fact that, by and large, nineteenth-century Westerners—missionaries and businessmen alike—probably saw more of the seamy sides of Chinese life and less of its better aspects than had their predecessors?

5. Finally, to what extent did it reflect a changing psychology in the West itself (nineteenth-century nationalism, racial intolerance, smug self-righteousness,

[18] Ricci, op. cit., pp. 86-88.

"the white man's burden," and so on) as contrasted with the greater cosmopolitanism of earlier centuries?

Irrespective of the weight we should attach to these or other factors, two general conclusions seem possible:

1. There is considerable evidence suggesting that China, prior to 1800, was in many respects—economic as well as cultural—equal to, or ahead of, the Western world. It has been estimated, for example, that as late as 1750 more books had been printed in China—the original home of printing—than in the rest of the world put together. This fact should be kept in mind by those who might be tempted to measure China's cultural tradition solely in terms of what has survived from it in recent times.

2. Throughout history China, to an unusual degree, seems to have been capable of inspiring either ardent admiration or intense antipathy. This fact is worth remembering now that China, as never before, has become—at least for Americans—a "controversial" subject.

3 The Language Problem

Language is an important factor in any cultural tradition. That is why, when studying a civilization other than our own, it is always pertinent to ask ourselves such questions as, To what extent can the distinctive ideas and institutions of the civilization in question be attributed to the influence of its language? In what ways has that language either aided or hindered the interchange of ideas with the outside world?

Such questions are easy to forget when studying a civilization which is linguistically and historically closely related to our own, such as ancient Rome. To "translate" Latin *spiritus* as English "spirit," for example, is obviously simple, and if the meaning of "spirit" is perhaps ambiguous in English, it is probably no more so than was its equivalent in the original Latin. At any rate, we have by so translating probably not greatly compounded the original ambiguity, since, in view of the common linguistic and historical roots of the two words, the ranges of ambiguity covered by *spiritus* and "spirit" are probably more or less the same.

As soon as we turn to utterly unrelated languages and civilizations, however, the problem becomes a great deal worse. *Shen,* for example, is the dictionary Chinese equivalent for English "spirit," but it by no means follows, in all or even most cases, that the two are identical in meaning. For not only do *shen* and "spirit," as words belonging to the philosophical and religious vocabulary, probably each possess more than one shade of meaning, but—which is much worse—these two ranges of meaning, owing to their diverse linguistic and historical backgrounds, probably only very imperfectly agree with each other. This is one of several reasons why, as so often happens, even reputable scholars can come up with widely different renditions of the same Chinese text.

A. MAJOR PRINCIPLES OF CHINESE

Much has been written about the Chinese language apropos the questions we have raised, but before these differing opinions can be intelligently considered, it is essential to have at least a minimal understanding of what the language itself is like. Fortunately, good treatises on the subject exist.[19] For reasons of space, however, we cannot quote them here but can only summarize in our own words a few features of basic importance (omitting entirely even such important matters as the question of tones or the alleged monosyllabism of Chinese):

1. Lack of Inflection

"Lack of inflection" means, for example, that the Chinese third personal pronoun *t'a* can mean "he, him, she, her, it"; the noun *ma* can mean either "horse" or "horses"; the verb *tsou* can mean "go, went, will go." And this in turn means that *context* is all important. Only by prefixing words like "one," "two," or "some" to *ma*, and "yesterday," "today," or "tomorrow" to *tsou*, can we know whether one or more horses are involved, and when the action takes place.

2. Word Order

Word order, as well as context, is very important because, in the absence of inflection, it is often only through grammatical position, as well as ideological context, that we can know how a word functions in a given sentence: as a noun, verb, or other part of speech. The single word *shang*, for example, can, depending on its position and context, variously function as a preposition (on, above, upon), an adverb (up, upward, above), an adjective (upper, high, superior, excellent), a noun (top, summit, a superior), or a verb (to mount, ascend, esteem). *Ma shang*, literally "horse-above," signifies "on horseback," whereas the reverse combination, *shang ma*, ordinarily means "to mount a horse." By putting the phrase into a different context, however, in which *shang* becomes an adjective instead of a verb, *shang ma* can equally well mean "superior or excellent horse(s)."

3. Primary and Secondary Meanings

Chinese words (as well as phrases) commonly have a primary meaning (which tends to be concrete), and, deriving from this, a series of secondary meanings which are often increasingly abstract or metaphorical. *Shang* as a verb, for example, primarily means "to ascend," but it also has the secondary meaning of "to esteem." *Ma shang*, primarily "on horseback," has a secondary but even more common idiomatic connotation of "immediately, at once." (The metaphor here is that of a person on horseback, poised to spring into action.) The primary meaning of *sheng* (not to be confused with *shang*) is "to produce, generate, give birth to"; deriving from this are such secondary meanings as "raw, unworked, fresh, new, unfamiliar, uncivilized." One of the many problems in reading Chinese is to determine which of several possible meanings best fits a given word or phrase in a given sentence.

4. Chinese Characters

Chinese characters, as is well known, consist of nonalphabetic graphs or symbols, each used to designate a single idea and a single spoken syllable, the pro-

[19] Brief, clear, and informative are the two books by a Swedish leader in the field, Bernhard Karlgren, *The Chinese Language* (New York: Ronald Press, 1949), and *Sound and Symbol in Chinese* (New York: Oxford University Press, 1923; reprinted 1946). Also good, but less easy for the layman, is R. A. D. Forrest, *The Chinese Language* (London: Faber & Faber, 1948). On the Chinese script, an admirable introduction is the pamphlet of H. G. Creel, *Chinese Writing* (Washington: American Council on Education, 1943).

nunciation of which, however, can vary according to the particular Chinese dialect in which it is being read. They are thus similar to our numerals 1, 2, 3, 4, which always retain the same meaning irrespective of how they are pronounced in different languages. The Chinese characters have been created according to several different principles, all of which, however, go back originally to simple pictographs or combinations of such pictographs; these in the course of time have become conventionalized or simplified into the forms current today. The char-

acter 木 , for example, is pronounced *mu* (in the standard northern dialect) and means "tree or wood"; it is the modern form of a pictograph showing a tree with roots and branches. (For the early form, see Plate 4, upper right.) By combining

one such tree with another, 林 , we obtain an entirely new character, *lin*, mean-

ing "grove or forest"; by tripling the trees we obtain 森 , pronounced *sen*

and meaning "luxuriant vegetation, jungle growth, overgrown." Likewise the

character *yin* 引 consists of a Chinese reflex bow on the left (see Plate 4, left

middle), and next to it a bowstring; its meanings include "to draw out, stretch, lead, guide, entice." Obviously, a script of this kind can more readily represent concrete objects than it can abstractions. Hence it reinforces the tendency of the language, already mentioned, to express the abstract and the intangible in terms of the concrete and the tangible.

5. *The Spoken and Written Languages*

Chinese contains an abundance of homonyms (syllables pronounced identically but having different meanings, such as English "to, too, two," "meat, meet, mete"). Were these to be used individually, they would, of course, create many verbal ambiguities. The spoken language avoids such ambiguities, however, by combining two syllables, similar in meaning, into a dissyllabic compound, and letting this compound stand for the idea which is common to both its components. The two syllables *yi* and *fu*, for example, both mean "clothing" (in addition to many other things); hence the spoken word for "clothing" becomes *yi-fu*, a compound which will not readily be confused by the ear for any other compound. When expressing the same idea in writing, however, this device is no longer needed, since every individual written character, regardless of its pronunciation, is *visually* distinct from every other character; hence it is necessary only to write the single character *yi*, meaning "clothing," or the single character *fu*, meaning the same, but not both of them put together (unless, of course, one were to write exactly as one would speak, but this, as we shall see, was not customary in the old China). It should be added that the above is only one of several explanations for the many compound terms found in Chinese. Other types also exist, such as *huo-ch'e*, literally "fire vehicle," which is the modern coined term for a railroad train.

Because of the above and other factors, too complex to be discussed here, a distinction early arose between Chinese as it is spoken and Chinese as it is written. Spoken Chinese, precisely because it was a spoken and therefore living language, underwent continuous evolution in the course of which it discarded old words, adopted new ones, and changed significantly in syntax. The more concise written medium, on the other hand, because of its separation from the living colloquial, froze at an early date into a relatively fixed form, stylistically and syntactically sharply different from the colloquial. So far apart, indeed, did the two become that even a native Chinese requires years of study to master the written language (also commonly known as literary or classical Chinese). And yet so great was the prestige of the literary language that until recently almost everything was written in it, aside from fiction and drama (which, for the very reason that they followed the colloquial idiom, were looked down on in traditional China).

6. *Characteristics of the Written Language*

A major characteristic of the written language, of course, is its telegraphic conciseness (half the length, as a rule, of a corresponding English translation; subjects of verbs, for example, are often unspecified and can only be inferred from the general context). Other features are the absence of punctuation (mitigated to some extent by conjunctions and similar words indicating a transition from one clause to another); the tremendous concern with stylistic balance and rhythm (likewise essential for determining punctuation; successive clauses tend to have the same number of characters, to be syntactically parallel to one another, and so on); the absence of any device (such as capitalization) for indicating proper names; and, finally, an overriding fondness for recondite literary allusions.[20]

Those same features of literary Chinese which give it its extraordinary vigor, beauty, and expressiveness also make it the despair of the translator. Probably the nearest English parallels—not in beauty, certainly, but in ambiguity, and then only to a very limited extent—are found in telegrams and newspaper headlines. Here, for example, is a headline the writer remembers seeing in the *New York Times*:

WAVES TO TRAIN IN MARYLAND

His immediate reaction was to ask himself: "Who the deuce was waving to the train, and why should this be news?" Only subsequently did he realize that he had confused the first word (a proper noun) for a verb, the third word (a verb) for a noun, and that what the headline was really trying to say was that the Waves (a female naval organization) were about to undergo training in Maryland.

B. THE CHINESE LANGUAGE AND CHINESE THINKING

With this by way of background, we are now ready to return to our initial question, in paraphrased form: "Has the Chinese language played a part in shap-

---

[20] Very occasionally in the old days texts were printed with rudimentary punctuation marks (dots and circles). These, however, were intended primarily for beginners and were scorned by true scholars. In recent decades, Western-style punctuation has become almost universal, with proper names often indicated by side lines or underlining.

ing prevailing patterns of Chinese thought?" Forrest, one of the latest writers on the subject, denies that there has been any appreciable influence:[21]

It is, I believe, a mistaken notion that differences of mentality can be deduced from differences in morphological form, syntax, or vocabulary. The last is certainly linked with the cultural stage and social interests of the speakers of the language; but it is the speakers who create the language in answer to their needs and develop new expressions as the occasions arise. . . . The principles of traffic safety are not essentially different in countries which drive to the right and in those which keep to the left; but it is essential that all drivers observe whatever convention is in use. It is just as idle to infer from peculiarities of Chinese vocabulary or word order a fundamental difference in that people's attitude to the external world as it would be to explain the various conventions of traffic control in the same way (pp. 76-77).

Even the least developed language is probably capable of expressing any ideas which its speakers may wish to express; and if it does not yet possess the means of expression for certain ideas, it is because the ideas themselves do not exist in the minds of its speakers. . . . A language is always sufficient to the needs of its speakers at any stage in their cultural history (p. 246).

Professor Dubs of Oxford, apropos the alleged influence of the language on Chinese philosophical thinking, has expressed a closely similar view:[22]

In spite of the many meanings of Chinese characters, if we have a sufficiently long passage, and if the *thought* of the author was clear, there is no necessary ambiguity. When we come to the field of philosophy, the ambiguity of European words is notorious. Such a word as "objective" or "subjective," "realism" or "idealism," often presents an insurmountable difficulty to clear thinking. . . . Yet the multitude of meanings of words does not necessarily produce ambiguity, because the context indicates which meaning is intended. . . . It is then false that the Chinese language is an inadequate vehicle for philosophical discourse because it does not possess an adequate supply of words or because these words are ambiguous (pp. 99-100).

Hence we have no reason to seek in the Chinese language the cause of the failure of the Chinese to develop such philosophical systems as those of Plato or Spinoza. The Chinese language is capable of expressing whatever ideas are desired to be expressed. Such expression may be more difficult than in a European language, but great Chinese thinkers, such as Hsüntzu, have made the Chinese language express their ideas precisely (p. 104).

Most other writers, however, strongly disagree. Several of them state specifically that Chinese is by nature better suited to poetry and other imaginative literature than to subjects requiring precision, like philosophy or science. Thus we are told by the late Marcel Granet, one of the most famous French scholars on China:[23]

The Chinese language appears to be in no way organized for the notation of concepts, analyses of ideas, or discursive exposition of doctrines. It is wholly

[21] Forrest, *op. cit.*, pp. 76-77, 246. It should be noted that Forrest probably has the spoken language primarily in mind, whereas the writers quoted later are probably thinking primarily of literary Chinese.
[22] H. H. Dubs, "The Failure of the Chinese to Produce Philosophical Systems," *T'oung Pao*, XXVI (Leiden, 1929), 99-100, 104.
[23] Marcel Granet, *La pensée chinoise* (Paris: Albin Michel, 1934), p. 82.

designed to communicate emotional attitudes, to suggest modes of behavior, to convince, to convert.

Similarly, the Dutch scholar Duyvendak, late professor of Chinese at Leiden:[24]

> The Chinese way of thinking is along concrete, descriptive, associative lines. As a type of language, Chinese shows a remarkable likeness to certain so-called "primitive" languages. It does not summarize, it does not analyse but it sees all things apart in never-ending variety. It accumulates one concrete simple image after another in the order in which they occur to the mind. It does not easily form comprehensive perceptions. . . . The concrete meaning of the words is strengthened and preserved by the ideographic character of Chinese writing. . . . A character denotes a complete idea without any limitation of word-categories, and consequently it leaves room for many associations.

I. A. Richards, the co-author of Basic English, is also author of an interesting study on types of reasoning in Mencius, in which he has this to say:[25]

> To a mind formed by modern Western training the interpretation of the Chinese Classics seems often an adventure among possibilities of thought and feeling rather than an encounter with facts (p. 1).

> We must often be doubtful whether Mencius (still more Confucius at times . . .) should not primarily be regarded as a poet. His aims seem often to be those of poetry rather than of prose philosophy. Be this as it may, his *method*—even when his method is severely prosaic—is frequently the method of condensed poetry. If we wished for a short description of the difference between Confucian philosophic method and, shall we say, Kantian, we could hardly do better than to say that the latter endeavours to use an explicit logic and the former an indicated guess (p. 7).

Victor Purcell, British colonial civil servant, makes the remark (very pertinent apropos the opinion of Dubs quoted above) that even if precision is *theoretically* possible in Chinese, the spirit of the language runs overwhelmingly against it:[26]

> The rule is, if you can possibly omit, do so. The result may be that the meaning is quite hidden, but the reader is supposed not only to have an encyclopaedic knowledge to assist him in his guess work, but to have unlimited time for filling in ellipses. This does not mean that the language has no words to fill in the ellipses, or that there are no words to convey tense, number, or mood. It merely means that the spirit of the language is against their use.

Not only Westerners but distinguished Chinese as well have voiced similar opinions, for example, the late diplomat Dr. W. W. Yen:[27]

> Chinese is a language more appropriate for the expression of poetic and literary fancies than for the conveyance of legal and scientific thought.

Likewise Achilles Fang, noted student of comparative literature:[28]

> In fact, "obscurity, erudition, allusiveness, . . ." as a critic in *Partisan Review* describes the modernist poetry of Europe and America, have always characterized Chinese literary style.

[24] J. J. L. Duyvendak, "A Literary Renaissance in China," *Acta Orientalia*, I (Leiden, 1923), 286-287.
[25] I. A. Richards, *Mencius on the Mind* (London: Kegan Paul, 1932), pp. 1, 7.
[26] Victor Purcell, *Problems of Chinese Education* (London: Kegan Paul, 1936), p. 93.
[27] Quoted in *ibid.*, p. 158.
[28] Achilles Fang, "Some Reflections on the Difficulty of Translation," in Arthur F. Wright, ed., *Studies in Chinese Thought* (Chicago: University of Chicago Press, 1953), p. 266.

On the related question of whether or not Chinese acts as a barrier to the interchange of ideas with other cultures, several of these scholars are equally positive. Richards, for example, tells us: "All the difficulties of translating Chinese into English are paralleled by the even worse difficulties in the reverse process." And further, concerning the need to create adequate Chinese equivalents for modern Western terms: "Few who have not been in close contact with Chinese students in China . . . can realize the gravity of the problem." [29]

Purcell's opinion is, if anything, even more pessimistic: "It is doubtful whether Chinese is capable of the exactness of expression requisite for scientific purposes." And he concludes: "It seems certain that for the purpose of teaching Western ideas, especially Western scientific ideas, the best course would be to adopt a Western language as a medium." [30]

A graphic summary of the whole problem has been given by Arthur Wright of Stanford: [31]

> Thus the monks from medieval India, the Jesuits from Renaissance Europe, emissaries of modern scientific thought such as Bertrand Russell, and representa· tives of the Comintern all spoke inflected polysyllabic languages. . . . Structurally Chinese was a most unsuitable medium for the expression of their ideas, for it was deficient in the notations of number, tense, gender, and relationships, which notations were often necessary for the communication of a foreign idea. . . . Moreover, Chinese characters as individual symbols had a wide range of allusive meanings derived from their use in a richly developed literary tradition. . . . Further, the Chinese was relatively poor in resources for expressing abstractions and general classes or qualities. Such a notion as "Truth" tended to develop into "something that is true." "Man" tended to be understood as "the people"— general but not abstract. . . . These characteristics of the Chinese language re- duced many proponents of foreign ideas to despair. . . . Kumarajiva (344-413), devoted Buddhist and stouthearted missionary, . . . was moved to sigh: "But when one translates the Indian [Buddhist texts] into Chinese, they lose their literary elegance. Though one may understand the general idea, he entirely misses the style. It is as if one chewed rice and gave it to another; not only would it be tasteless, but it might also make him spit it out."

C. CHINESE LANGUAGE REFORM TODAY

The features of literary Chinese whose effects we have been discussing—use of a script intended for the eye rather than the ear, divorce from the living collo- quial, refractoriness to ideas of foreign origin—have combined to make it enor- mously potent as an instrument for maintaining Chinese cultural continuity. This it has done along two major lines:

> 1. It has given to China an unexampled literary and hence cultural *continuity in time,* inasmuch as an educated Chinese could, once he possessed a knowledge of the written language, read ancient classics, written thousands of years ago, with little less facility than contemporary documents. This meant that the early classics came to be revered as the highest models of style and thought, and ex- erted a profound and uninterrupted influence upon countless generations of Chinese scholars.

[29] Richards, *op. cit.*, pp. 126, 127-128.
[30] Purcell, *op. cit.*, pp. 156, 160.
[31] Arthur F. Wright, "The Chinese Language and Foreign Ideas," in Wright, ed., *op. cit.*, p. 287

2. It also gave to China an equally striking literary and cultural *unity in space*. For though many of the dialects spoken in China differ from each other as widely as do English and French, yet the domination of the literary classical language prevented the emergence of regional types of literature, and so assured a means of communication that was equally accessible to every literate Chinese.[32]

With the growing pressure for modernization in the last half century, however, the literary language has come to be viewed by Chinese reformers, no longer as a valued conserver of past tradition, but as a formidable barrier to needed change. The result has been a series of attempts at language reform, beginning in 1917 with that known as the *pai-hua* movement. This was the movement to replace the literary language entirely by a new written medium based in vocabulary and syntax upon the Chinese colloquial language, known as *pai-hua* (literally, "white— i.e., plain or undecorated—speech"). Its significance has been described by John Fairbank of Harvard as follows:[33]

> ın the twentieth century a script and even a vocabulary which had been largely created about the time of Christ were still being used. In the minds of Western educated Chinese it inevitably became a question whether this language, like Latin in the West, had not become outmoded and insufficient for modern needs. . . . The first stage in the linguistic revolution was to use the everyday vernacular speech in written form—the step taken in Europe at the time of the Renaissance, when the national vernaculars supplanted Latin. In China leadership was taken by the noted scholar and writer who later became known to Americans as China's wartime ambassador, Dr. Hu Shih. While a student at Cornell during World War I he had advocated the use of the *pai-hua*, or Chinese spoken language, as a written medium for scholarship and all purposes of communication. Many others joined in this revolutionary movement, which denied the superior value of the literary style. . . . The use of *pai-hua* spread rapidly, carrying with it the acknowledgment that the tyranny of the classics had been broken.

Written *pai-hua*, despite its unquestioned superiority to the classical language for expressing modern concepts, depends, like the latter, upon the age-old characters, of which the student must memorize four or more thousand, some of them requiring twenty or more strokes to write. Not surprisingly, therefore, the Chinese Communists have recently promulgated two further reforms of epoch-making significance. The first, already in operation, is a systematic simplification of the forms of the more cumbrous and common characters. It, however, is merely preliminary to the second much more revolutionary step, that of replacing the characters entirely by an alphabet. When this change will begin is, as of this writing (1957), unknown, other than that it will not come soon and will be introduced only very gradually. It is already announced, however, that the new script will, for purely linguistic reasons, be based on the Latin and not the Russian alphabet.

The momentousness of this step can hardly be overemphasized. Attempts to alphabetize Chinese, to be sure, are by no means new; they began in the early

---

[32] D. Bodde, "The Chinese Language as a Factor in Chinese Cultural Continuity," in *Far Eastern Leaflets, Numbers 1-6* (Washington: American Council of Learned Societies, 1942), p. 29. Similar statements have been made by many scholars, for example, Karlgren, *The Chinese Language*, pp. 57-58.

[33] Reprinted by permission of the publishers, from John K. Fairbank, *The United States and China* (Cambridge, Mass.: Harvard University Press, 2nd rev. ed., 1958), pp. 168–169. Copyright 1948, 1958, by the President and Fellows of Harvard College.

nineteenth century with certain Western missionaries and were then sporadically
continued by Chinese reformers. In the absence of strong government support,
however, they were all inevitably doomed to failure.[34]

Even today, with the backing of a powerful dictatorship, the difficulties, both
technical and psychological, are such as to dwarf those faced by Ataturk when
he alphabetized Turkish in the 1920's. Technically speaking, Dr. De Francis is
surely right when he stresses "the linguistic dictum that whatever can be spoken
intelligibly can be written phonetically." [35] The alphabetization of *pai-hua*, in
other words, is technically feasible *if* (and this is a big if) persons are willing to
write in it *exactly* (or very nearly exactly) as they would speak (in other words,
without using literary phrases from the classical language such as now often
occur in written *pai-hua*). Whether future writers can or will restrict themselves
in this way, however, remains the big question. Should the effort prove successful, it would probably mean the gradual disappearance, or at least drastic curtail-
ment, of China's many local dialects, in favor of a standard *lingua franca* (based
on the present Peking dialect).

When we turn to the classical literature, the problems faced, because of its
innumerable ambiguous homonyms, become much more serious. "The conclusion
. . . that they cannot be alphabetized . . . ," writes De Francis, "is to be reached
for virtually all materials published in the classical literary style." [36] In other
words, alphabetization would apparently mean the loss of some three thousand
years of classical literature for all future generations save a few specialists who
might continue to study it, very much as Greek and Latin are studied in the West
today. Conceivably, to be sure, selected works could be "translated" into modern
alphabetized *pai-hua*, but these, in view of the sheer bulk of the extant literature,
could probably never be more than a small proportion of the total.

No wonder, then, that Karlgren wrote more than thirty years ago:[37]

> If China does not abandon its peculiar script in favour of our alphabetic
> writing, this is not due to any stupid or obdurate conservatism. The Chinese
> script is so wonderfully well adapted to the linguistic conditions of China that
> it is indispensable; the day the Chinese discard it they will surrender the very
> foundations of their culture.

No wonder, either, that the Communist program has been attacked from For-
mosa as "nothing less than the drastic elimination of the Chinese language and
the repudiation of all traditional Chinese learning." [38] To this the Communist
reply is that literacy—and with it modernization—is impossible for a population
of almost 600 million without alphabetization. Furthermore, regarding the classical literature, the situation will be no worse than it has always been, since never
in the past was the written language understood by more than 10 or 15 per cent
of the population.

[34] The authoritative work on this subject is John De Francis, *Nationalism and Language Reform
in China* (Princeton, N. J.: Princeton University Press, 1950).
[35] *Ibid.*, p. 184.
[36] *Ibid.*, pp. 184-185.
[37] Karlgren, *Sound and Symbol in Chinese*, p. 41.
[38] *Chung-yang Jih-pao* (Central Daily News), February 5, 1956, as quoted by Tao-tai Hsia,
"The Language Revolution in Communist China," *Far Eastern Survey*, XXV (October, 1956),
154.

Dr. Hsia of Yale concludes his informative and objective article on the subject as follows:[39]

> We may be critical of many things that the Communist Government is doing but we must realize that language reform in China is closely linked with the expansion of literacy, a threshold crossed by all advanced countries. Dr. Hu Shih, whose thinking has been constantly assailed in Communist China, and other intelligent Chinese educators, saw the need many years ago of a language revolution if China was to be set on the path of progress. . . . The present language campaign on the Chinese mainland, although obviously initiated with the intention of aiding Communist rule, will, like the earlier language movement led by Dr. Hu Shih, also bring knowledge to many of the Chinese people and in some respects make their life richer. The disappearance of old style aesthetic Chinese characters will indeed be a loss to world culture, but it may be more than outweighed by the advantages the revolutionized language will bring.

POSTSCRIPT

On July 8, 1957, after this book had gone into composition, the *New York Times* carried a not altogether clear dispatch from its Hong Kong correspondent, Tillman Durdin, reporting a radical reversal in the alphabetization program. "Last year," wrote Mr. Durdin, this program "appeared to have been virtually decided," but "faced with the actuality of the change, . . . opposition began to manifest itself. Scholars trained in both the Western and Chinese cultures of the pre-Communist era began to question the wisdom of the reform, which some said was based on the ideas of ardent but inexperienced revolutionaries."

In Peking, ten days earlier, Durdin's dispatch continued, the secretary general of the Committee for the Reform of Writing informed two French students visiting China that the Chinese characters were not to be abandoned after all, and that it was planned to use romanization only for teaching children and illiterates the correct pronunciation of the characters, as well as providing a uniform phonetic transcription for China's many dialects. "Chinese characters . . . are eternal," the secretary general is reported to have said, "and there is no question that . . . the present form of writing be suppressed or even altered." As of this writing it remains uncertain whether this informal pronouncement really represents a definitive policy decision or not. If it does, there is no doubt it marks a striking victory for Chinese tradition.

[39] Tao-tai Hsia, *loc. cit.* For another good exposition, see Harriet C. Mills, "Language Reform in China: Some Recent Developments," *Far Eastern Quarterly*, XV (1956), 517-540. Beginning with the sixteenth volume (1956-1957) this periodical was renamed the *Journal of Asian Studies*.

B. THE WORLD OF THE SUPERNATURAL

In the following sections we shall be examining the Chinese cultural tradition under three main headings: the world of the supernatural, the world of nature, and the world of man. In other words, what have been the major Chinese approaches to religion, to the physical universe, and to themselves?

1 The Chinese Attitude toward Religion

Much misunderstanding about Chinese religion has arisen from translation of the word *chiao* as "religion," without further qualification. Confucianism, Taoism, and Buddhism, for example, are commonly said to be the "three *chiao*" or "religions" of China. Here is what the noted scholar Hu Shih has to say about this key term:[40]

> The Chinese word for "religion" is *chiao* which means teaching or a system of teaching. To teach people to believe in a particular deity is a *chiao*; but to teach them how to behave toward other men is also a *chiao*. The ancients did say that "the sages founded religions (*chiao*) on the way of the gods." But it is not always necessary to make use of such supernatural expedients. And the Chinese people make no distinction between the theistic religions and the purely mortal teachings of their sages. Therefore, the term *chiao* is applied to Buddhism, Taoism, Mohammedanism, Christianity, as well as Confucianism. They are all systems of moral teaching. Teaching a moral life is the essential thing; and "the ways of the gods" are merely one of the possible ways of sanctioning that teaching. That is in substance the Chinese conception of religion.

Are then Confucianism, Taoism, and Buddhism to be accounted religions in the usual Western sense? Concerning the first, Chinese opinion is overwhelmingly in the negative. Lin Yutang says, for example, "Confucianism, strictly speaking, was not a religion: it had certain feelings toward life and the universe that bordered on the religious feeling, but it was not a religion." [41] Likewise, we are told by Wing-tsit Chan of Dartmouth, in his informative study of modern Chinese religion: "Confucianism is . . . certainly not a religion in the Western sense of an organized church. . . . To this day, the Chinese are practically unanimous in denying Confucianism as a religion." [42]

Not only does the noted philosopher and historian of Chinese philosophy, Fung Yu-lan, concur; he further points out that even Taoism and Buddhism, though they exist as organized religions, also exist as noninstitutionalized systems of philosophy:[43]

[40] Hu Shih, *The Chinese Renaissance* (Chicago: University of Chicago Press, 1934), p. 79.
[41] Lin Yutang, *My Country and My People* (New York: John Day, 1935), p. 105.
[42] Wing-tsit Chan, *Religious Trends in Modern China* (New York: Columbia University Press, 1953), p. 16.
[43] Fung Yu-lan, *A Short History of Chinese Philosophy*, ed. D. Bodde (New York: Macmillan, 1948), pp. 1, 3. Reprinted with the permission of The Macmillan Company.

Confucianism is no more a religion than, say, Platonism or Aristotelianism. It is true that the *Four Books* have been the Bible of the Chinese people, but in the *Four Books* there is no story of creation, and no mention of a heaven or hell. . . . As to Taoism, there is a distinction between Taoism as a philosophy . . . and the Taoist religion. . . . Their teachings are not only different; they are even contradictory. . . . As to Buddhism, there is also a distinction between Buddhism as a philosophy . . . and Buddhism as a religion.

Even in the case of the institutionalized religions, moreover—in other words, those having an organized clergy, ritual, dogma, and pantheon—we find the Chinese attitude to them very different from that usual in the West. This distinction has been graphically pointed out by the anthropologist Francis Hsu of Northwestern University as follows:[44]

It is completely inaccurate to describe the Chinese—as social scientists, historians and missionaries have done—as Buddhists, Taoists, Confucianists or ancestor worshippers in the same sense that we classify Americans as Jews, Protestants or Catholics. The American *belongs* to a church or temple, provides for its support, attends its services and goes to its social meetings. Protestant differentiation, in turn, compels him to be a Presbyterian or a Baptist. Yet he must not only be a Baptist, but most choose between being a Northern Baptist or a Southern Baptist. Finally he is not only a Northern Baptist, but he is known also as a member of the First Baptist Church or the Third Baptist Church of Jonesville, Ohio. . . .

The Chinese tendency is exactly the reverse. The Chinese may go to a Buddhist monastery to pray for a male heir, but he may proceed from there to a Taoist shrine where he beseeches a god to cure him of malaria. Ask any number of Chinese what their religion is and the answer of the majority will be that they have no particular religion, or that, since all religions benefit man in one way or another, they are equally good.

In short, the Chinese attitude toward religion is eclectic:

For the last fifteen hundred years, the three systems [Confucianism, Taoism, Buddhism] have been mutually penetrated, interrelated, and partially identified. They have become 'three roads to the same destination,' as the Chinese people are fond of saying.[45]

This failure of Chinese religion to develop either into a single universal church or into several rigidly exclusive sectarian churches possibly goes back to the fact that, from earliest times, ancestor worship has predominated above all other forms of religious expression:[46]

The dominance of this [ancestral] cult probably goes far to explain one of the most striking differences between early China and many other civilizations: the absence in the former of a universal church or a significant priesthood. For this there is a two-fold explanation. In the first place, the ancestral sacrifices of each clan were necessarily offered only to its clan ancestors, not to those of any other clan. Secondly, these sacrifices, in order to be effective, had to be performed by the clan members in person, not by priestly proxies. As a result, the ancestral

---

[44] Francis L. K. Hsu, *Americans and Chinese: Two Ways of Life* (New York: Abelard-Schuman, 1953), p. 237.
[45] Chan, *op. cit.*, pp. 180-181.
[46] D. Bodde, "Authority and Law in Ancient China," in *Authority and Law in the Ancient Orient*, Supplement No. 17 (1954), *Journal of the American Oriental Society*, p. 47.

cult was inevitably divisive rather than unifying in its effects. It could not readily develop into a national religion with a powerful organized priesthood.

A second factor was the absence of personality in early Chinese religion. Aside from the ancestors themselves (who were spirits of the departed rather than actual gods), what the ancient Chinese worshiped or propitiated were objects and forces of nature, such as mountains, rivers, the rain and wind, and the life-giving soil. Even the highest divinity of all, T'ien, or Heaven, though originally anthropomorphic, rapidly became depersonalized into an abstract ethical power or (in some contexts) became secularized entirely into the nonreligious name for the physical sky (a meaning the word *t'ien* still holds in modern Chinese). For this reason there was in ancient China no elaborate pantheon or mythology, no heaven (as a place of reward for the blest) or hell, no story of creation, and no theory of divine retribution after death. All these phenomena became conspicuous only in imperial times, probably as a result of the advent of Buddhism.

Does this then mean that the Chinese are indifferent to religious matters? Though many people have asserted as much, Hu Shih denies it vigorously, particularly for certain periods:[47]

> I wish to point out that it is entirely wrong to say that the Chinese are not religious. No people is really incapable of religious life or experience. But there is always a difference in definitions. And there is always a vast difference in the degree of religiosity or piety (p. 78).

> There were long periods in Chinese history when this people also became so fanatically religious that a pious monk would burn a finger, or an arm, or the whole body, willingly and devoutly, as the supreme form of devotion in his Buddhist faith. There were times when every fourth man in the population would be a Buddhist monk or a Taoist priest. There were times when the court and the people spent millions of ounces of silver yearly to build grand temples and monasteries, and millions of acres of land were donated to the monasteries as voluntary offerings to the gods (p. 80).

Significantly, however, Dr. Hu's remarks apply almost entirely to one long but single age in China: that of Buddhist domination (very roughly, A.D. 300-900). Ever since that time Buddhism (and with it the other organized religions) has been declining in China; prior to it, moreover, China produced a golden age of philosophy but very little in the way of organized religion. Taoism, for example, flourished for centuries as a philosophy before one branch of it—inspired, at least in part, by Buddhist example—evolved into an institutionalized church having a dogma, pantheon, and clergy. Taking Chinese history as a whole, therefore, there is evident truth in Wing-tsit Chan's remark: "It is amazing how few religious leaders China has produced." [48] And even Hu Shih himself is forced to admit, though with primary reference to the modern scene: "It is true that the Chinese are not so religious as the Hindus, or even as the Japanese; and they are certainly not so religious as the Christian missionaries desire them to be." [49]

Underlying this situation is the basic absence from Chinese thinking of any monotheistic concept of deity—a point to which we shall return in a later section (F, 1). Professor Hsu suggests that there is a correlation between Chinese poly-

[47] Hu, *The Chinese Renaissance*, pp. 78, 80.
[48] Chan, *op. cit.*, p. 138.
[49] Hu, *op. cit.* p. 78.

theism and emphasis on the group, on the one hand, and between Western monotheism and emphasis on the individual, on the other:[50]

> Christianity and Judaism, the two monotheistic religions which are the most
> popular in the West, are essentially religions of the individual. They emphasize
> a direct link between the one and only God and the individual human soul. The
> more fervent is the worshipper's belief in individual self-reliance, the stronger is
> his faith that there is only one omnipresent, omnipotent and even omniscient . . .
> God. This being the case, by definition all other gods are false and evil idols to be
> eliminated at whatever cost.

> On the other hand, in a society where human relationships are inclusive rather
> than exclusive, and which are shared rather than monopolized, the worshipper
> finds polytheism to his liking. This religious outlook encourages not only a belief
> in many gods, but it emphasizes the co-existence of all supernatural beings. . . .
> The usual aim of the believer is to establish a satisfactory relationship with all
> spiritual forces, and the open and avowed reason is the achievement of specific
> human ends. Thus as man's activities extend and his purposes multiply, his gods
> become more numerous. In the minds of Chinese believers there is therefore no
> question of which gods are true and which false.

2 Religious Persecution in China

Everything we have been saying would seem to suggest that the Chinese have
been remarkably free from religious bigotry. And such indeed has been the opinion reached by countless Westerners ever since the good Bishop Andrew, in the
fourteenth century, commented on what he termed the "erroneous view [of the
Chinese], that everyone can find salvation in his own religion." [51] At the beginning of the present century, however, the well-known Dutch scholar de Groot
produced a large two-volume work to refute this view, in the introduction to
which he wrote:[52]

> A chimera has to be banished from our minds and to make room for the con-
> viction that we approach a good deal nearer to the truth by admitting the Chinese
> State to be the most intolerant, the most persecuting of all earthly governments;
> a State which, on account of certain ancient dogmatic principles in the system of
> political philosophy whereon it is based, could not consistently do otherwise than
> brandish fire and sword in the face of every religious community or sect which,
> since the days of Confucius, has ventured to make its appearance in China.

Before leaping to conclusions, it is well to evaluate the writer's psychology by
reading his earlier lines (p. 2), in which he describes the civilizing work of the
Christian mission abroad and its centuries-old respected status at home:

> The mission, an institution which in our social system has for centuries en-
> joyed full civic rights and the sympathy of tens of thousands of individuals, . . .
> the mission, deserving of respect on account of its spirit of self-sacrifice for the
> good of its heathen fellow-creatures, on account of its endeavours to raise these

---

[50] Hsu, *op. cit.*, pp. 236-237.
[51] See Sect. A, 2. In speaking thus disparagingly of the very factor that made it possible for him
to preach Christianity in China, Andrew was of course revealing his own typically Western
point of view. For subsequent confirmations of Chinese religious tolerance, see the remarks of
Pereira and Ricci, quoted in the same section.
[52] J. J. M. de Groot, *Sectarianism and Religious Persecution in China* (2 vols.; Amsterdam:
Johannes Müller, 1903-1904), I, 3.

less civilized elements of mankind to a higher standard . . . —this institution surely deserved a better treatment.

There is no doubt that de Groot is correct in pointing out that serious persecutions have occurred in China, notably against Buddhism in 446, 574, 845, and 955, but also against other religions, including Christianity. Of them all, unquestionably the greatest was that of 845, resulting in the destruction of no less than 4,600 large Buddhist monasteries, more than 40,000 smaller ones, the return of some 260,000 monks and nuns to lay life, and confiscation of enormous amounts of church land.

On the other hand, it should first of all be noted that these persecutions were all conducted solely by the government, were not participated in by the general population, did not lead to religious wars, and were rarely of long duration (that of 845 was revoked within a year). In the second place, and more important, their motivation was less doctrinal than it was economic or political. Secret religious societies, for example, were frequently proscribed, not at all because they were religious, but because they were often antidynastic. What Edwin Reischauer of Harvard says about the persecutions of Buddhism applies, with minor variations, to the other persecutions as well:[53]

> It would be a mistake to think of Buddhist persecutions in China in terms of the relentless conflict between Christian and Mohammedan in the West or of the fratricidal strife and inquisitions within Christianity. There has been very little religious conflict in China, compared with Western Asia or Europe, and what religious persecutions have occurred have been motivated more by secular than by strictly religious reasons. Throughout Chinese history the chief cause for overt opposition to Buddhism has been economic rather than religious. As we have seen, Chinese administrators deplored the fact that monasteries not only removed good lands from the tax registers, but also sheltered able-bodied monks who otherwise would support the economy of the state by paying taxes and performing other services.[54]

Though there has been a good deal more religious intolerance in China than most people probably suspect, it is very likely also true that most Western scholars, in the light of our own religious history, would agree with Francis Hsu in his remark:

> When one compares this kind of persecution with the kind that has characterized the great monotheistic religions of the West he is left with the feeling that if the latter are tragic dramas in the classic mold the Chinese affairs are but one act trifles.[55]

3 Religion of the Masses and of the Intellectual

It is more clearly in religion than in any other field that differences between China's educated minority and its illiterate majority appear. Indeed, as pointed

[53] Edwin O. Reischauer, *Ennin's Travels in T'ang China* (New York: Ronald Press, 1955), p. 218.
[54] For a detailed account of the economic factors leading up to the 845 persecution, see Kenneth Ch'en, "The Economic Background of the Hui-ch'ang Suppression of Buddhism," *Harvard Journal of Asiatic Studies*, XIX (1956), 67-105.
[55] Hsu, *op. cit.*, p. 248.

out by Wing-tsit Chan, these differences are far more important than those traditionally noted between Confucianism, Taoism, and Buddhism:[56]

> I have always urged that instead of dividing the religious life of the Chinese people into three compartments called Confucianism, Buddhism, and Taoism, it is far more accurate to divide it into two levels, the level of the masses and the level of the enlightened. . . . The masses worship thousands of idols and natural objects of ancient, Buddhist, Taoist, and other origins, making special offering to whatever deity is believed to have the power to influence their lives at the time. The enlightened, on the other hand, honor only Heaven, ancestors, and sometimes also Confucius, Buddha, Lao Tzu, and a few great historical beings, but not other spirits. The ignorant believe in the thirty-three Buddhist heavens, eighty-one Taoist heavens, and eighteen Buddhist hells. . . . As is well known, belief in Heaven and Hell was unknown in Chinese history until Buddhism introduced it into China. The enlightened Chinese flatly reject such belief. The masses believe in astrology, almanacs, dream interpretations, geomancy, witchcraft. . . . The enlightened are seldom contaminated by these diseases.

Turning first to the popular side, we find the imperial age, following the advent of Buddhism, characterized by a growing proliferation of gods, spirits, and demons. We have seen, for example (Sect. A, 1), how, according to religious Taoism, the human body is populated by no less than 36,000 deities. These supernatural beings have varied enormously according to time, place, and group. Each craft guild, for example, had its own deified founder, important to itself but not to others; each city had its own protective God of Walls and Moats, commonly a deified local hero. Other deities, on the other hand, enjoyed more generalized popularity, such as Chung K'uei, the demon chaser (see Plate 1). All of them, however, whether local or national, somewhere found a place in a vast interlocking spirit hierarchy which, as Francis Hsu has pointed out, very closely paralleled the hierarchy of men on earth:[57]

> The Chinese world of the spirits is essentially like their world of men. In each the mass of common men are governed by a hierarchy of officials. . . . The Supreme Ruler of Heaven has jurisdiction over all men and all gods. . . . But he was not omnipresent. In this regard he differs fundamentally from the Christian God. To govern both gods and men, the Supreme Ruler depends upon a large number of functionaries who have titles and ranks not unlike those of officials under the emperor. . . .
>
> It is not solely the structure of the Chinese world of the spirits that is similar to the world of men. The presumed attitudes of the gods toward men and the actual attitudes of men toward their gods are equally reflective of the relationship between Chinese dynastic rulers and their subjects. As in their dealings with worldly officialdom, the Chinese respect their gods, but they keep their distance from them—they feel neither identification with them nor emotional attachment to them.

Toward these popular beliefs a small segment of China's intellectuals has always expressed attitudes ranging from amused condescension to outright contempt. We have already quoted (Sect. A, 1), for example, the argument of the

---

[56] Chan, op. cit., pp. 141-142.
[57] Hsu, op. cit., pp. 220-222. This world of spirits, with its human foibles and weaknesses, has been delightfully satirized in the great sixteenth-century Chinese novel partially translated by Arthur Waley as Monkey (New York: John Day, 1944).

first-century iconoclast Wang Ch'ung against the immortality of the soul. Wang's skepticism, in actual fact, has much earlier roots. On the one hand, it derives from the naturalism of philosophical (as opposed to religious) Taoism, exemplified, for instance, in the saying of Lao Tzu (*ca.* 300 B.C.): "Heaven and Earth are not benevolent; for them the myriad creatures are but straw dogs." [58] On the other hand, it is rooted in the humanistic skepticism of Confucianism, as typified, for example, by Hsün Tzu (*ca.* 298-*ca.* 238): [59]

> If people pray for rain and get rain, why is that? I answer: There is no other reason for it. It is simply as if there had been no prayer for rain, and it had nevertheless rained. When people . . . pray for rain in a drought, or when they decide an important affair only after divination, this is not because they think in this way they will get what they want, but only to make a fine appearance. Hence the Superior Man looks upon it as a fine gloss put over the matter, while the common people consider it supernatural.

In recent times Confucian humanism and Taoist naturalism have combined with modern science to produce a view of life termed by Wing-tsit Chan the "religion of the intellectual." Here, in his own words, are some of its salient features: [60]

> The ultimate goal of religion, then, is man's moral perfection. Religion is therefore essentially ethical and social. This emphasis leaves no room for fanatic and mystical experience. Any abnormal practices like asceticism, celibacy, and self-immolation are ruled out. . . . While faith, piety, and meditation are of great value, the basic way to salvation is morally good life and good society (pp. 248-249).

> Fulfillment of human nature is the way to serve Heaven, for the simple reason that individual nature is identical with universal nature. What is endowed in man is of the same essence as the true nature of the entire universe. . . . As Chang Tung-sun has pointed out, "The concept of all things forming one body has been a persistent tendency in Chinese thought from the beginning to the end." . . . It is not an exaggeration to say that it represents the common belief of Chinese intellectuals (p. 253).

The following are typical statements from prominent present-day Chinese intellectuals. The first is from the philosopher Fung Yu-lan: [61]

> When people get rid of religion and have no substitute, they also lose the higher values. . . . Fortunately, however, besides religion there is philosophy, which provides man with an access to the higher values—an access which is more direct than that provided by religion, because in philosophy, in order to be acquainted with the higher values, man need not take the roundabout way provided by prayers and rituals. . . . [These values] are even purer than those acquired through religion, because they are not mixed with imagination and superstition. In the world of the future, man will have philosophy in the place of religion. . . . It is not necessary that man should be religious, but it *is* neces-

---

[58] See Lao Tzu, *Tao Te Ching,* Chap. 5. Dogs of straw were used in sacrifice, but when the sacrifice was over they were cast aside.
[59] See trans. of Dubs (here modified), *The Works of Hsüntze,* pp. 181-182.
[60] Chan, *op. cit.,* pp. 248-249, 253.
[61] Fung, *A Short History of Chinese Philosophy,* pp. 5-6

sary that he should be philosophical. When he is philosophical, he has the very best of the blessings of religion.

The second statement is from Lin Yutang:[62]

There is religion as a sanction for moral conduct: here the Chinese and the Christian points of view differ widely. Humanist ethics is a man-centered, not a God-centered ethic. To the West, it seems hardly imaginable that the relationship between man and man (which is morality) could be maintained without reference to a Supreme Being, while to the Chinese it is equally amazing that men should not, or could not, behave toward one another as decent beings without thinking of their indirect relationship through a third party. . . .

There is [also] religion as an inspiration and living emotion, a feeling for the grim grandeur and mystery of the universe. . . . There are moments in our lives . . . when we live more than the life of the senses and we look over the visible world to the Great Beyond. These moments come to the Chinese as to the Europeans, but the reactions are decidely different. It has seemed to me, formerly a Christian and now a pagan, that though religion gives peace by having a ready-made answer to all these problems, it decidedly detracts from the sense of the unfathomable mystery and the poignant sadness of this life, which we call poetry. Christian optimism kills all poetry. A pagan . . . is driven inevitably to a kind of pantheistic poetry. . . . To the West, . . . religion seems the natural escape. But to the pagan, this religion seems to be based on the fear that there is not enough poetry and imagination in this present life to satisfy the human being emotionally.

The third statement, from Hu Shih, is a short excerpt from a ten-point personal credo which, when he enunciated it in 1921, had a profound effect on fellow intellectuals:[63]

We should recognize that the universe and everything in it follow natural laws of movement and change—"natural" in the Chinese sense of "being so of themselves"—and that there is no need for the concept of a supernatural Ruler or Creator. . . .

We should recognize the terrific wastefulness and brutality in the struggle for existence in the biological world, and consequently the untenability of the hypothesis of a benevolent Ruler. . . .

We should recognize that the individual self is subject to death and decay, but the sum total of individual achievement, for better or worse, lives on in the immortality of the Larger Self [humanity as a whole]; that to live for the sake of the species and posterity is religion of the highest kind; and that those religions which seek a future life either in Heaven or in the Pure Land [of Buddhism], are selfish religions.

Whether or not statements such as these can be said to constitute a "religion" depends, of course, upon one's own religious outlook. Dr. Hu, on the one hand, flatly asserts that "practically all the prominent leaders of thought in China today are openly agnostics and even atheists." [64] Professor Chan, on the other, maintains that "modern intellectuals . . . do not believe in spirits as they are understood

[62] Lin, op. cit., pp. 106-107.
[63] Hu Shih, "My Credo and Its Evolution," in Albert Einstein et al., Living Philosophies (New York: Simon & Schuster, 1931), pp. 260-261.
[64] Hu, The Chinese Renaissance, p. 78.

by the ignorant masses. But there is no doubt that they believe in a power above physical existence." [65]

4 Chinese Religion Today

When Wing-tsit Chan visited China in 1948-1949, just before the triumph of Communism, what he saw of the organized religions was discouraging:[66]

> For several hundred years, no important [Buddhist] scripture or commentary has been written. The clergy is notoriously ignorant and corrupt. Temples are either in poor state of preservation or saturated with an atmosphere of commercialism (p. 54).

> The first thing that strikes us is the general decline of the folk religion. Thousands of images have been smashed. Priests, monks, and nuns have been driven out of temples. Temples have been used for nonreligious or even anti-religious purposes or have been confiscated or destroyed (p. 145).

> It is generally considered that Taoism as a religion is already defunct. This is not to say that there are no more temples, shrines, idols, or priests, . . . but the real spirit of the religion is dead (p. 146).

Can religions such as these offer any effective challenge to such a dynamic ideology as Marxism? To ask the question is to answer it. What then about the "religion of the intellectual"? By many it is asserted that Confucian humanism, from which it receives so much, cannot conceivably co-exist with Marxism. Chan, however, expresses a contrary point of view, and his reasons for so doing are worth pondering:[67]

> Since it is profoundly rationalistic and naturalistic, it should be easy for it to get along with a philosophy [Marxism] that prides itself on its scientific attitude. Humanism in Chinese religion should have no quarrel with an ideology that professes to stand for the welfare of the masses. Since there is no organization in this religion, there will be no conflict between the church and the state. And since it is essentially a private philosophy of life, it will be largely immune from governmental control.

Aside from the final sentence, which seems unduly optimistic in view of the all-embracing nature of Communism, there would appear to be considerable substance to this statement.

What then about Christianity, a religion of which we have heretofore said nothing? On the one hand, Christianity has enjoyed a prestige and influence in modern China out of all proportion to its size. Yet, on the other, its Chinese converts, by the 1930's, numbered less than four million (very much under 1 per cent of the total population), despite a history of intermittent missionary activity going back to the Nestorian Christians of the seventh century. Many reasons for this slow growth should be apparent from the preceding pages. To them Chan adds a further factor which he regards as vital:[68]

[65] Chan, op. cit., p. 255.
[66] Ibid., pp. 54, 145, 146.
[67] Ibid., pp. 262-263.
[68] Ibid., pp. 260-261.

Few mature Chinese intellectuals have been converted to Christianity, . . . partly due to the intellectuals' distaste for belonging to any particular religion, and partly due to the lack of communication between Chinese intellectuals and Christianity. . . . So long as foreign religions fail to come in contact with the Chinese intelligentsia, they will have failed to reach the nerve center of the Chinese people. . . . How certain Christian doctrines, such as incarnation, atonement, and sin, can be presented to Chinese intellectuals is a real problem. Realizing its great difficulty, Francis Wei, a Chinese Christian leader, urges concentration on the greatness of Jesus instead of on doctrinal presentation. This is wise counsel, for the inspiring power and exemplary character of Jesus, like much of the good work done by the church in education and medicine, is generally and favorably accepted by the Chinese intellectuals.

It is significant that the inspiring character of Jesus, together with the doing of good works, is precisely what the Chinese Christian church is emphasizing today, now that, under Communism, it has perforce lost its foreign contacts and become a wholly Chinese-supported and oriented institution. Can it survive in its new isolated environment? Or will it, as twice before in Chinese history, gradually fade from the scene? It would be foolhardy to attempt an answer at this time.[69]

One final question remains to be asked: Communism, because of its fanaticism, exclusiveness, and similar qualities, has often been likened to a militant religion. Inasmuch, however, as these are precisely the qualities which have failed to appeal to Chinese during most of their history, is it likely that they will seem any more attractive today when presented in a new Communist dress? Most Americans would probably answer no. In 1949, however, not long after watching the Communists march triumphantly into Peking, the present writer had this to say:[70]

> The present movement has sent its roots down into China's masses in a way the Kuomintang [the Nationalist Government of Chiang Kai-shek] never was able to do. . . . Moreover, it comes to power at a time when China's social and economic disintegration is much further advanced, and people therefore psychologically ready to turn to radical solutions which they would otherwise shun. History shows that in the past, during periods of stress, the Chinese have been ready to embrace ideas which, in normal times, they would have rejected as "un-Chinese."
>
> One such period was that of the Warring States (fifth to third centuries B.C.), when the reformer Mo Tzu and his followers tried to solve the political and social crisis of their day through methods that seemed dangerously radical to their contemporaries. . . . Another such period was that of the civil wars and barbarian invasions from the third to the fifth centuries A.D., when people shunned the responsibilities of society by seeking refuge in the new Buddhist church, some chopping off fingers or even burning themselves alive in their eager fervor to gain salvation.
>
> Both movements died, but the real reason, I think, is that neither of them ever really changed the fundamental political and economic fabric of Chinese society. . . . Today, however, the situation is different. The Communists possess both a dynamic ideology and the political power to make it effective.

[69] For two interesting accounts of Christianity in Communist China, see Gerald Bailey, "Out of Red China," *The Christian Century*, November 30, 1955, pp. 1393-1395, and Francis P. Jones, "The Christian Church in Communist China," *Far Eastern Survey*, XXIV (December, 1955), 184-188.

[70] D. Bodde, *Peking Diary: A Year of Revolution* (New York: Abelard-Schuman, 1950), pp. 148-149.

It is Chan's opinion that "Communism may change Chinese religion, but Chinese religion may change Communism too." [71] This statement accords with general theories of acculturation, and some observers have indeed believed that they detected a certain moderation and flexibility in the Chinese form of Communism, such as could perhaps be attributed to the influence of Chinese tradition. Here, for example, is the opinion expressed by a man who recently became one of America's first newspapermen to enter Communist China since 1949, and who had previously been a correspondent in Moscow for *Look* magazine:[72]

> Thus the [Chinese Communist] regime has a far broader base of popular support than any other Communist government, including that of the Soviet Union. This gives it flexibility and independence. . . . This much is certain: The Chinese have already demonstrated a degree of flexibility and realism far superior to that shown by other Communists. And it is dangerous wishful thinking to suppose that they could be overthrown by a military excursion from Formosa.

The great question remains, however, which of the two components—the alien or the indigenous—will in the long run change more and along what lines.

[71] Chan, *op. cit.*, Preface, p. x.
[72] Edmund Stevens, "Inside Red China," *Look*, XXI, No. 8 (April 16, 1957), 36.

C. THE WORLD OF NATURE

1 The Taoist View of Nature

Between this and the preceding section there is a continuity, for there we were primarily concerned with religion as a formalized institution, whereas here our concern is with an attitude to nature which, though it admits of no theology, no pantheon, and no church, is nevertheless essentially religious in quality. In this attitude concerning man's position in the total universe—for that is what it really is—we find the mainspring for much of China's literature and art. From the famous poet T'ao Ch'ien (372-427), for example, there is the following:[73]

> I built my hut in a zone of human habitation,
> Yet near me there sounds no noise of horse or coach.
> Would you know how that is possible?
> A heart that is distant creates a wilderness round it.
> I pluck chrysanthemums under the eastern hedge,
> Then gaze long at the distant summer hills.
> The mountain air is fresh at the dusk of day:
> The flying birds two by two return.
> In these things there lies a deep meaning;
> Yet when we would express it, words suddenly fail us.

And here is a shorter poem by Liu Tsung-yüan (773-819), one of the literary giants of the T'ang dynasty (618-906):[74]

> A hundred mountains and no bird,
> A thousand paths without a footprint;
> A little boat, a bamboo cloak,
> An old man fishing in the cold river-snow.

During the Sung dynasty (960-1279), when Chinese painting reached its apogee, the art critic Kuo Hsi (born *ca.* 1020) wrote a famous *Essay on Landscape Painting* in which he began:[75]

> Why does a virtuous man take delight in landscapes? It is for these reasons: that in a rustic retreat he may nourish his nature; that amid the carefree play of streams and rocks, he may take delight; that he may constantly meet in the country fishermen, woodcutters, and hermits, and see the soaring of the cranes, and hear the crying of the monkeys. The din of the dusty world and the locked-in-ness of human habitations are what human nature habitually abhors; while, on the contrary, haze, mist, and the haunting spirits of the mountains are what human nature seeks, and yet can rarely find. . . .

---

[73] Reprinted from *Translations from the Chinese* by Arthur Waley, p. 83, by permission of Alfred A. Knopf, Inc. Copyright 1919, 1941 by Alfred A. Knopf, Inc. Reprinted by permission, also, of George Allen & Unwin Ltd.
[74] Reprinted from *The Jade Mountain* by Witter Bynner and Kiang Kang-hu, p. 97, by permission of Alfred A. Knopf, Inc. Copyright 1929 by Alfred A. Knopf, Inc.
[75] See Shio Sakanishi, trans., *An Essay on Landscape Painting* (London: Murray, 1935), pp. 30-31.

Having no access to the landscapes, the lover of forest and stream, the friend of mist and haze, enjoys them only in his dreams. How delightful then to have a landscape painted by a skilled hand! Without leaving the room, at once he finds himself among the streams and ravines; the cries of the birds and monkeys are faintly audible to his senses; light on the hills and reflection on the water, glittering, dazzle his eyes. Does not such a scene satisfy his mind and captivate his heart? That is why the world values the true significance of the painting of mountains.

Throughout Chinese poetry and painting we find this same awareness of the beauty and mystery of Nature—always, however, a Nature in which man holds an integral but not assertive place. Never, on the one hand, are the mountains, rivers, and forest of the great Chinese landscape painters mere decorative backdrops for man and his activities, as so often in preromantic Western art; equally never, on the other hand, do they consist simply of empty and seemingly uninhabited wildernesses. Always they are peopled by human figures, tiny yet distinct: a fisherman in his boat, a woodcutter, a cowherd, a recluse sitting in contemplation on a rock. (See Plate 2.) So too in the paintings of animals, birds, insects, and plants, in which the Chinese excel: always these creatures must be shown *alive* and in their natural surroundings; never as the string of slaughtered game, the platter of plucked fruit, the bowl of cut flowers so beloved by the Western painter of still life. (See Plate 3.)

With this Chinese attitude toward nature it is instructive to compare the attitudes found in the premodern West. Concerning the Greeks and Romans we are told by Irving Babbitt, for example:

Nature interests them as a rule less for its own sake than as a background for human action; and when they are concerned primarily with nature, it is a nature that has been acted on by man. They have a positive shrinking from wild and uncultivated nature.

Concerning the Middle Ages:

No man who knows the facts would assert for a moment that the man of the Middle Ages was incapable of looking on nature with other feelings than those of ascetic distrust. It is none the less true that the man of the Middle Ages often saw in nature not merely something alien but a positive temptation and peril of the spirit. In his attitude towards nature as in other respects Petrarch [1304-74] is usually accounted the first modern. He did what no man of the mediaeval period is supposed to have done before him, or indeed what scarcely any man of classical antiquity did: he ascended a mountain out of sheer curiosity and simply to enjoy the view.

And concerning the age of neoclassicism:

An age that aims first of all at urbanity must necessarily be more urban than rural in its predilections. . . . Wild nature the neo-classicist finds simply repellant. Mountains he looks upon as "earth's dishonor and encumbring load." The Alps were regarded as the place where Nature swept up the rubbish of the earth to clear the plains of Lombardy.[76]

[76] Irving Babbitt, *Rousseau and Romanticism* (Boston: Houghton Mifflin, 1919), pp. 270, 272-274. Apropos Babbitt's reference to urbanity, it is instructive to note that our word "civilization" goes back to a Latin root having to do with citizen and city, whereas the Chinese equivalent, *wen-hua*, literally means "the transforming influence of literature." For us, in other words, the prime factor in civilization is urbanization; for the Chinese, it is the art of writing.

Even with the coming of romanticism, the Western approach to nature never really coincided with that of the Chinese. For though it expressed genuine love for nature, it also commonly sought to exalt human personality by demonstrating man's command over nature. In China, on the other hand, people have been climbing mountains from times immemorial simply because it was natural and pleasing to them to do so; no one, however, would ever have dreamed of ascending an Everest because by so doing he would achieve what no man had ever achieved before.

The roots of the attitude we have been describing lie in philosophical (not religious) Taoism, and it is in this philosophy that we must look for the imaginative, spontaneous, and poetic aspects of the Chinese mind—the rich results of which, in art and literature, would be well worth exploring in detail if space permitted.[77] Here, for example, is the way Chuang Tzu (ca. 369-ca. 286 b.c.) describes what he calls "Earth's music":[78]

> The breath of this Great Lump [the terrestrial earth] is called the wind. At times it remains inactive, but when it acts, angry sounds come forth from every aperture. Is it only you, then, who has not heard its growing roar? The imposing forms of the mountain forest, the apertures and cavities in huge trees many a span in girth: these are like nostrils, like mouths, like ears, like beam sockets, like goblets, like mortars, like pools, like puddles. Into them goes the wind, making sounds of rushing water, of whizzing arrows, of scolding, of breathing, of shouting, of crying, of deep wailing, of moaning agony. Some sounds are shrill, some deep. Gentle winds produce minor harmonies; violent winds, major ones. When the fierce gusts pass away, all the apertures are empty and still. Is it only you, then, who has not seen the bending and quivering of the branches and leaves?

And here is Chuang Tzu's allegory of the autumn floods:[79]

> It was the time when the autumn floods come down. A hundred streams swelled the River, that spread and spread till from shore to shore, nay from island to island, so great was the distance that one could not tell horse from bull. At this the God of the River felt extremely pleased with himself. It seemed to him that all lovely things under heaven had submitted to his power. He wandered down-stream, going further and further to the east, till at last he came to the sea. He gazed eastwards, but could discern no end to the waters. Then this God of the River began to turn his head, peering this way and that, till at last, addressing the God of the Sea, he said with a deep sigh: "There is a proverb which says, 'Though of teachings one hundred he has heard, yet in them he finds nothing equal to himself.' I fear this indeed applies to me. "

The relativity of all things, symbolized by this story, leads naturally to Chuang Tzu's mysticism, as expressed in his famous anecdote of himself and the butterfly:[80]

---

[77] The best introductions to Chinese art and literature are, respectively, those of Laurence Sickman and Alexander Soper, *The Art and Architecture of China* (Baltimore: Penguin, 1956), and James Robert Hightower, *Topics in Chinese Literature: Outlines and Bibliographies* (Cambridge, Mass.: Harvard University Press, 1950).
[78] Trans. of Fung Yu-lan (slightly modified), *Chuang Tzu* (Shanghai: Commercial Press, 1933), pp. 43-44.
[79] Trans. of Arthur Waley (slightly modified), *Three Ways of Thought in Ancient China* (London: Allen & Unwin, 1939), pp. 55-56.
[80] Fung (slightly modified), *Chuang Tzu*, p. 64.

> Once I, Chuang Chou, dreamt of being a butterfly; a butterfly that flitted hither and thither, enjoying itself as it wished. Nor did it know that it was Chuang Chou. But suddenly, awakening, there, amazingly, was Chuang Chou. Now know I not: Is it really Chuang Chou who was dreaming he was a butterfly? Or is it the butter-fly dreaming it is Chuang Chou?

It is very doubtful whether many farmers, Chinese or otherwise, would think of themselves as butterflies. And yet there is a very real connection between this kind of thinking and the lives of those innumerable inarticulate and illiterate peasants who have always formed the basis of the Chinese social pyramid. For, whereas Greek philosophy sprang from the mercantile life of the Greek city states, Chinese philosophy, like Chinese society generally, has always been rooted in the soil. In the words of Fung Yu-lan:[81]

> Although the "scholars" did not actually cultivate the land themselves, yet since they were usually landlords, their fortunes were tied up with agriculture. A good or bad harvest meant their good or bad fortune, and therefore their reaction to the universe and their outlook on life were essentially those of the farmer. In addition their education gave them the power to express what an actual farmer felt but was incapable of expressing himself. This expression took the form of Chinese philosophy, literature, and art. . . . Taoism and Confucianism . . . are poles apart from one another, yet they are also the two poles of one and the same axis. They both express, in one way or another, the aspirations and inspirations of the farmer.

2 Chinese Cosmological Thinking

Besides the Taoist approach to nature, there is another which is less poetic, more mechanistic, perhaps more "scientific," and which centers around the cosmological theories associated with the Yin and Yang and the Five Elements. The Yin and Yang are the two primary principles, or forces, of the universe, eternally inter-acting with each other, yet at the same time eternally opposed. With them many qualities and things are correlated, including the following:

Yang principle: brightness, heat, dryness, hardness, activity, masculinity, Heaven, sun, south, above, roundness, odd numbers.

Yin principle: darkness, cold, wetness, softness, quiescence, femininity, Earth, moon, north, below, squareness, even numbers.

Just as all life results from the interactions of male and female, so all universal phenomena result from the interactions of these two cosmic principles. Yet it is evident from the early graphs for the words (rainclouds for the Yin, sunrays for the Yang) that meteorological conditions and not the sexual analogy dominated the minds of the unknown originators of the Yin-Yang conception. Even today, in fact, the meteorological associations remain strong. The alternation of day and night, the ebb and flow of the tides, and, above all, the yearly round of the seasons through alternating phases of heat and cold, light and darkness, growth and decay: all these represent the Yin and Yang in their eternal interplay. In this cosmic symphony neither the one nor the other ever permanently triumphs; each grows from the other and needs the other as its partner in order to generate the

---

[81] Fung, *A Short History of Chinese Philosophy,* pp. 18-19.

universe as we find it. That is why, in the Yin-Yang symbol which occurs frequently in Chinese art, a black dot appears within the light-colored Yang, symbolic of the embryonic Yin, and a light dot within the dark-colored Yin, symbolic of the embryonic Yang.

The Yin-Yang Symbol

That this concept is still alive in the modern Far East is shown by the fact that the Yin-Yang symbol forms the central emblem on the flag of the Republic of South Korea. Curiously enough, it has also crossed the Pacific to this country to become the insignia of the Northern Pacific Railroad.

Though the Yin and Yang definitely complement each other, Chinese thinkers nevertheless generally agree that the former is always subordinate to the latter. Tung Chung-shu (179?-104? B.C.), for example, regards the inequality between the two as cosmic justification for the inequalities within the human social order. "The ruler," he writes, "is Yang, the subject Yin; the father is Yang, the son Yin; the husband is Yang, the wife Yin." [82] In this insistence on mutual reciprocity coupled with mutual inequality, we come upon one of the most conspicuous themes in Chinese philosophical thinking:

> Chinese philosophy is filled with dualisms in which, however, their two component elements are usually regarded as complementary and mutually necessary rather than as hostile and incompatible. A common feature of Chinese dualisms, furthermore, is that one of their two elements should be held in higher regard than the other. Here . . . , therefore, we have an expression of the [prevalent Chinese] concept of harmony based upon hierarchical difference.[83]

It is important, therefore, to distinguish between this Chinese kind of dualism and the superficially similar dualisms of light and darkness, good and evil, God and the Devil, and so on, common to the ancient Near East and to our own Western world. The latest of several scholars to call attention to this difference is the British historian of Chinese science, Joseph Needham of Cambridge University:[84]

> Another very common suggestion has been that the Yin-Yang dualism of Chinese thought . . . was an importation of Iranian origin. Originally meaning the "shady side" and the "sunny side" of hills or houses, the words suddenly appear as philosophical terms about the 4th century B.C., Yin standing for dark, weak, female, night, moon and so on; and Yang standing for bright, strong, male, day, sun, etc.—from these categories an elaborate theory of Nature grew up. A superficial similarity with Zoroastrianism is obvious, but I entirely agree with Waley in

[82] Quoted in Fung Yu-lan, *A History of Chinese Philosophy*, trans. D. Bodde (2 vols.; Princeton, N. J.: Princeton University Press, 1952-1953), II, 42-43.
[83] D. Bodde, "Harmony and Conflict in Chinese Philosophy," in Arthur F. Wright, ed., *Studies in Chinese Thought* (Chicago: University of Chicago Press, 1953), p. 54.
[84] Joseph Needham, *Science and Civilisation in China* (2 vols. to date; New York: Cambridge University Press, 1954, 1956), I, 153-154.

his rejection of any direct influence. "In Zoroastrianism," he says, "darkness is essentially evil; the principle of light, essentially good. But the fundamental conception of Yin and Yang was quite different; they were two independent and complementary facets of existence, and the aim of the Yin-Yang philosophers was not the triumph of light, but the attainment in human life of perfect balance between the two principles." [85]

It is instructive to compare this conception with the vulgarization that developed within religious Taoism, in which, as pointed out by Schuyler Cammann of the University of Pennsylvania, the Yin came to be regarded as a positive force for evil: [86]

> By the later Han dynasty [A.D. 25-220], . . . the mystical strain [in early Taoism] began to be replaced by another with a great emphasis on magic. The latter soon evolved into a popular faith much concerned with the pursuit of long life, . . . and with means for procuring release from evil influences that were thought to be generated by the Yin principle. For these magical-minded Taoists, the Yang and the Yin, instead of representing the active and passive forces of nature in harmonious relationship, had come to be considered as the very essence of good and evil, respectively. . . .

> Diseases and the evil spirits who strove to shorten the span of life were also believed to be embodiments of the Yin. Thus, anything associated with the opposing Yang principle was believed to have great power as a counteracting force and demon-repellant. For this reason, anything colored red (the Yang color) was considered as especially auspicious. . . .

> The evil forces of Yin were collectively expressed in the early Taoist iconography by small demons, or *kuei,* and an even more demoniac figure, by the name of Chung K'uei, was devised to keep the latter in check. Until recent years his picture alone was considered a powerful symbol for exorcising evil.

A look at our Plate 1 should convince any reader of Chung K'uei's efficacy as a demon repeller.

Returning to the Chinese cosmologists, we find that the theories of the Five Elements hold quite as important a place in their thinking as those connected with the Yin and Yang. These Five Elements consist of wood (symbolic of plant growth), fire (essence of the Yang), earth or soil, metal, and water (essence of the Yin). Through the interactions of the Yin and Yang, matter comes to be differentiated into the Five Elements; these in turn interact to produce the multiplicity of existing things, all of which, therefore, pertain to one or another of the elements, or represent varying combinations of them. Here, then, we find yet another conspicuous characteristic of the Chinese mind: that termed by Joseph Needham *correlative thinking.* By this phrase he means its tendency to group all things and ideas, natural and human alike, into neatly arranged sets of numerical categories, among which those in fives, owing to the importance of the Five Elements, are by far the most numerous. The following are a very few of the main correlations in five: [87]

---

[85] Needham is here quoting from Arthur Waley, *The Way and Its Power* (London: Allen & Unwin, 1934), p. 112.
[86] Schuyler Cammann, "Types of Symbols in Chinese Art," in Wright, ed., *op. cit.,* pp. 214-216.
[87] Tables similar to the following (but sometimes considerably more elaborate) can be found in many works, for example, Alfred Forke, *The World-Conception of the Chinese* (London: Probsthain, 1925), pp. 240-241.

Five Elements	Four Seasons	Five Directions	Five Animals	Five Creatures	Five Grains	Five Organs	Five Numbers	Five Colors	Five Tastes	Five Smells
wood	spring	east	sheep	scaly	wheat	spleen	8	green	sour	goatish
fire	summer	south	fowl	feathered	beans	lungs	7	red	bitter	burning
earth	———	center	ox	naked	panicled millet	heart	5	yellow	sweet	fragrant
metal	autumn	west	dog	hairy	hemp	liver	9	white	acrid	rank
water	winter	north	pig	shell-covered	millet	kidneys	6	black	salt	rotten

Each element assists the operations of the particular season of which it is the correlate, thus acting, so to speak, as a localized subaltern of the Yin and Yang, which operate equally through all the seasons. Unfortunately for the cosmologists, however, nature provided them with only four seasons to go with five elements. Yet they ingeniously managed to overcome this difficulty, some by assigning earth, as the "central" element, to all the seasons equally rather than to any one of them, others by arbitrarily converting the third month of summer into an artificial "fifth" season, to which they assigned earth.

In the field of history, likewise, the Five Elements were assigned to successive epochs, though in a different sequence, beginning with earth, then followed by wood (wood grows out of earth), metal (metal cuts wood), fire (fire melts metal), water (water extinguishes fire), and so back to earth again (earth dams up water). Here we find one example of a widespread Chinese historical view which sees all history in terms of endlessly recurring cycles. Common to all these cyclical theories, of course, is that, unlike evolutionary theories of the modern West, they deny all possibility of progressive movement toward a higher level.

3 Man as the Correlate of Nature

This correlative thinking, distant in spirit though it be from Chuang Tzu's dream of the butterfly, rests like the latter on the conviction of the essential oneness of Man and Nature. How painfully literal this conviction could become in the hands of some of the correlative thinkers, the following summary well illustrates:[88]

> The universe with its dual forces [the Yin and Yang] is a macrocosm. Man is a microcosm, a little universe. Thus we read that as heaven is round and the earth square, so a man's head is round and the feet square. As heaven has its sun and moon, its order of stars, rain and wind, thunder and lightning, so man has two eyes, a set of teeth, joy and anger, voice and sound. The earth with its mountains and valleys, rocks and stones, trees and shrubs, weeds and grasses, has its parallel on the human body in the shoulders and armpits; nodes and tuberosities; tendons and muscles; hairs and down. The four limbs correspond to the four seasons; the twelve joints to the twelve months. . . . The pulse is of twelve kinds to agree with the twelve rivers. The heart contains seven holes because the ursa major is composed of seven stars, and the human skeleton has 360 bones for the simple reason that there are the same number of degrees in a circle.

[88] K. Chimin Wong and Wu Lien-teh, A History of Chinese Medicine (2nd ed.; Shanghai: National Quarantine Service, 1936), p. 21.

The close interrelationship of the human and natural worlds means that disturbances in the one result in corresponding disturbances in the other. Floods, droughts, plagues, and innumerable other abnormal phenomena are thus positive evidence of irregularities in human society. Many curious beliefs along these lines have been recorded for us, notably by the skeptic Wang Ch'ung, who lived in an age (the first century A.D.) when this kind of thinking was most popular:[89]

> The school of changes and reversions says that the eating of grain by insects is caused by officials of the various departments. Out of covetousness they make encroachments, and this results in the insects eating the grain. When these latter have black bodies and red heads, it is said to be the military officials [who are to blame], whereas when they have black heads and red bodies, then it is said to be the civil officials. When punishment is brought to those officials whom the insects resemble, these insects thereupon disappear and are no longer seen.

One of the major functions of the ruler is to maintain the cosmic balance between man and nature, and this he does not only by governing well but also through correct ritualistic behavior (in which sympathetic magic often finds a place). Thus we are told by John Fairbank:[90]

> The emperor's position was midway between the mass of mankind and . . . Heaven. It was his function to maintain the all-important harmony between them. This he did first of all in a ritualistic manner, by conducting sacrifices like those performed annually until a short time ago at the Altar of Heaven in Peking, and by a multitude of other ceremonial acts. . . . Any failure in the emperor's ceremonial observances was soon likely to be manifest in an irregularity of natural processes. Ceremonial conduct was therefore all-important.

Though among sophisticated people the literal belief in the more bizarre expressions of this cosmic magic gradually weakened, among the masses it has persisted until recent times, perpetuated in good part by religious Taoism. The Yin-Yang and Five Elements theories, too, have remained basic to traditional astronomy, medicine, biology, and naturalistic studies generally. Here, for example, is the way in which the Yin and Yang classifications continued to be applied in traditional medicine:[91]

> In medicine everything is classed under the two main divisions [the Yin and Yang]. On the human body, the skin or surface is Yang, the interior Yin; the back is Yang, the abdomen Yin. . . . Of the five viscera, the heart and liver are Yang organs and the spleen, lungs and kidneys are Yin organs. . . . A disease is Yang when it is due to external causes and Yin when it is from internal causes. So fever, affections of the upper body, respiratory diseases . . . are Yang diseases. Chills, affections of the lower body, circulatory diseases . . . are Yin diseases. . . . Even drugs have this distinction. Stimulants . . . and hot decoctions are classified as Yang drugs. Astringents . . . and cold infusions are Yin drugs.

Curiously enough, Chinese medicine is today enjoying something of a renaissance in Communist China, where new- and old-style doctors reportedly work

---

[89] See trans. of Forke (here modified), *Lun Heng*, II, 363.
[90] John K. Fairbank, "Tributary Trade and China's Relations with the West," *Far Eastern Quarterly*, I (1942), 131.
[91] Wong and Wu, *op. cit.*, p. 19.

together in harmonious cooperation. This cooperation exists, not, obviously, because the Communists believe in the Yin and Yang or Five Elements but rather because it has been demonstrated empirically that many of the old remedies actually work. Other factors, no doubt, are the insufficiency of Western-trained doctors for the new enlarged medical program, as well as the general Communist policy of reawakening Chinese pride in China's cultural past (exemplified by the revival of folk arts, music, and the like).

4 Chinese Naturalism and Science

We do not propose to discuss here, important though they be, such products of Chinese technology as paper, printing, porcelain, gunpowder, the crossbow, the magnetic compass, and a host of other lesser-known inventions, the transmission of which to Europe, usually many centuries later, often profoundly affected the course of civilization there.[92] Rather we are interested in the relationship of the naturalistic thinking we have been discussing to scientific methodology and ways of thought. Along what lines, then, has this Chinese naturalism influenced indigenous Chinese scientific development, and to what extent is it compatible with modern science today? On the second of these questions the veteran educator Chiang Monlin has written very perceptively:[93]

> Chinese morals are derived from nature; Christian morals from divine power; for the Chinese the gods are but part of nature, while to Christians nature is but the creation of God. On these grounds it is plain that the conflicts between Christian dogma and science were bound to be very serious, as Western history has proven in abundance; while the conflicts between science and Chinese moral precepts would be mild since both started from the same ground—nature—only traveling in different directions.

There is little doubt that this statement would be heartily seconded by the leading Western historian of Chinese science, Joseph Needham, who in the second volume of his opus (dealing with the intellectual background of Chinese science) has written at length on the scientific role of Taoism. Here we can quote only brief excerpts:[94]

> The Taoist system of thought, which still today occupies at least as important a place in the background of the Chinese mind as Confucianism, was a unique and extremely interesting combination of philosophy and religion, incorporating all "proto"-science and magic. It is vitally important for the understanding of all Chinese science and technology. According to a well-known comment (which I remember hearing from Dr. Fung Yu-lan himself at Chengtu), Taoism was "the

[92] The major—indeed only—comprehensive work on Chinese technology and science generally is that of Joseph Needham (see footnote 84), of which two of the seven projected volumes have already appeared. For popular pamphlets discussing Chinese inventions, products, and ideas, and their influence on the West, see D. Bodde, *China's Gifts to the West* and *Chinese Ideas in the West* (Washington: American Council on Education, 1942 and 1948, respectively).
[93] Chiang Monlin, *Tides from the West: A Chinese Autobiography* (New Haven, Conn.: Yale University Press, 1947), p. 252.
[94] Needham, *op. cit.*, Vol. II: *History of Scientific Thought*, pp. 33, 47.

only system of mysticism which the world has ever seen which was not profoundly anti-scientific" (p. 33).

Nothing is outside the domain of scientific inquiry, no matter how repulsive, disagreeable, or apparently trivial it may be. This is a really important principle, for the Taoists, who were orienting themselves in a direction which would ultimately lead to modern science, were to have to take an interest in all kinds of things utterly disdained by the Confucians and their descendants—in seemingly worthless minerals, wild plants and animal and human parts and products. (p. 47).

Elsewhere Dr. Needham contrasts this attitude with that of the Buddhists, whose rejection of the sensory world, he points out, inevitably made them indifferent to science. This statement, no doubt, is true, yet it also seems true that, as pointed out by the present writer in a review of Needham's book, the very attitude toward nature which encouraged the Taoists to study natural phenomena at the same time prevented their studies from going beyond a certain point:[95]

Needham is . . . unfavorable in his evaluation of Buddhism. The acceptance of Nature is, as he points out, an essential prerequisite for any scientific progress, and this of course was impossible for the Buddhists, for whom the sensory world is only *maya* or illusion. It is perhaps worth adding here, however, that an *uncritical* acceptance of Nature may be almost as harmful to science as an attitude of total rejection. What is needed is a middle course: one that accepts Nature but at the same time examines it with detachment. And this the Taoists (at least the mystical Taoists) could not provide, owing to their organismic view of the universe, which caused them to seek absorption into Nature, rather than to stand apart and measure it from the outside.

Needham himself, in fact, seems to recognize this in a later passage, in which, after stressing the great scientific achievements of the Taoists, he is nevertheless forced to conclude:[96]

Unfortunately, they failed to reach any precise definition of the experimental method, or any systematisation of their observations of Nature. So wedded to empiricism were they, so impressed by the boundless multiplicity of Nature, so lacking in Aristotelian classificatory boldness, that they wholly dissociated themselves from efforts . . . to elaborate a logic suitable for science. Nor did they realise the need for the formation of an adequate corpus of technical terms.

If this criticism be true of the Taoists, what then about the Yin-Yang and Five Elements cosmologists, who certainly *did* make efforts to classify this "boundless multiplicity"? In view of the absurdities to which their theories sometimes led them, we might expect Needham's opinion to be unfavorable, but this is by no means so:[97]

We must consider for a moment the five-element theories from the more practical point of view as a help or a hindrance to the advance of the natural sciences. They may seem odd to the modern scientific mind approaching them without reflecting on the history of science in Europe. In the hands of the adepts they attained absurdities but these were no worse than medieval European theorising

[95] D. Bodde, "Needham on Chinese Science and Philosophy," *Journal of Asian Studies*, XVI (1957), 265.
[96] Needham, *op. cit.*, II, 161-162.
[97] *Ibid.*, 293.

on elements, stars and humours. Looking back on all the foregoing, the five-element and Yin-Yang system is seen to have been not altogether unscientific.

This judgment finds some confirmation in what the Polish-British scientist Bronowski—speaking with particular reference to the astronomer Kepler—has to say about the workings of the creative mind in science:[98]

> Kepler's mind, we know, was filled with just such fanciful analogies; and we know what they were. Kepler wanted to relate the speeds of the planets to the musical intervals. He tried to fit the five regular solids into their orbits. None of these likenesses worked, and they have been forgotten; yet they have been and they remain the stepping stones of every creative mind. . . . To us, the analogies by which Kepler listened for the movements of the planets in the music of the spheres are far-fetched; but are they more so than the wild leap by which Rutherford and Bohr found a model for the atom in, of all places, the planetary system?

A few paragraphs further on, here is the way Bronowski describes the aim of science:

> All science is the search for unity in hidden likenesses. . . . The progress of science is the discovery at each step of a new order which gives unity to what had long seemed unlikely. . . . Science is nothing else than the search to discover unity in the wild variety of nature—or more exactly, in the variety of our experience.

Such a unity was certainly what the Chinese cosmologists, with their numerous correlations, were looking for. Their failure, however, lay in a scholasticism which neglected to check these correlations against the actual world of physical reality. Of the prominent Five Elements theorist Tung Chung-shu, for example, we are told that for three whole years he was so occupied with books that he did not even bother to look out into his garden.[99] This anecdote, though quite possibly apocryphal, well typifies much of the spirit of the movement. In the West, of course, a similar scholasticism long prevailed, but there, as pointed out by Needham, changes occurred which finally destroyed it:[100]

> The only trouble about the Chinese five-element theories was that they went on too long. What was quite advanced for the first century was tolerable in the eleventh, and did not become scandalous until the eighteenth. The question returns once again to the fact that Europe had a Renaissance, a Reformation, and great concomitant economic changes, while China did not.

Why China did not experience these changes is a fascinating subject which unfortunately cannot be adequately treated in this book, though we shall revert to it in our closing pages. At this point we can only agree with Needham's contention that between Chinese correlative thinking and Chinese social and political organization a relationship certainly existed:[101]

> Chinese society was a bureaucratism (or perhaps a bureaucratic feudalism), i.e. a type of society unknown in Europe. The point to be made is that . . . [Chinese

---

[98] J. Bronowski, "Science and Human Values," *The Nation* (December 29, 1956), p. 552 and (for the following quotation) pp. 553-554.
[99] Fung, *A History of Chinese Philosophy,* II, 16.
[100] Needham, *op. cit.,* II, 294.
[101] *Ibid.,* 337.

correlative thinking] . . . might be regarded as in a sense the heavenly counterpart of the bureaucracy upon earth, the reflection upon the world of Nature of
the particular social order of the human civilization which produced it.

The time has now come for us to examine the characteristics of Chinese society
and of the Chinese state.

PLATE 1. Chung K'uei, the Demon Chaser. Ink on paper. Attributed by the seal (probably falsely) to the Shun-chih Emperor (1644-61), founder of the Ch'ing dynasty, who was also a painter. (Author's collection)

PLATE 2. "Fishing in a Mountain Stream." By Hsü Tao-ning (fl. 11th century). Detail of a scroll, ink on silk. (Courtesy William Rockhill Nelson Gallery of Art, Kansas City)

"With united calls the frost-bringing geese are talking;
Along twin banks the reed-brakes reach their autumn."

PLATE 3. By the Buddhist monk Shih-t'ao (*ca.* 1630–*ca.* 1714). From an album, ink on paper.
Dated in a cyclical year corresponding to 1707. (Author's collection)

EARLY	MODERN	MEANING AND EXPLANATION	EARLY	MODERN	MEANING AND EXPLANATION
		Cliff			Tree, wood (*tree with roots and branches*)
		Mouth			To compare (*file of 2 men*)
		Enclosure			Hair, feathers (*piece of fur or down*)
		Evening, dusk (*crescent moon*)			Grass (*growing plants*)
		Large (*frontal view of "large" man*)			Insect, reptile (*snake or worm*)
		Child, boy (*child with upraised arms*)			To see (*exaggerated eye on legs*)
		To lift, greet (*joined hands*)			Speech (*vapor or tongue leaving mouth*)
		Bow (*Chinese reflex bow*)			Eating vessel (*vessel on pedestal*)
		Heart, mind (*picture of physical heart*)			Feline, reptile (*cat-like animal*)
		Door, house (*left leaf of double door*)			Fish
		Hand (*showing five fingers*)			Birds
		To beat, tap (*hand holding stick*)			Hemp (*hemp plants drying under shed*)
		Sun			Toad
		To speak (*mouth with protruding tongue?*)			Sacrificial urn (*two-handled tripod vessel*)
		Moon, month			Drum (*drum on stand; hand with stick*)

PLATE 4. Early and Modern Forms of Chinese Pictographs. Other Chinese characters can be much more complex than these. The "early" forms are in many cases not the earliest known. The "modern" ones became current around the first century A.D. (Adapted from Raymond D. Blakney, *A Course in the Analysis of Chinese Characters*, Peiping, 1948)

D. THE WORLD OF MAN

1 The Family System

Throughout the world, of course, the family has always been basic to society, but in China it became elaborated to such a point that we may fairly speak of it as *the* Chinese family system." What this signified has been summarized as follows by Fung Yu-lan:[102]

> The family system was the social system of China. Out of the five traditional relationships, which are those between sovereign and subject, father and son, elder and younger brother, husband and wife, and friend and friend, three are family relationships. The remaining two, though not family relationships, can be conceived of in terms of the family. Thus the relationship between sovereign and subject can be conceived of in terms of that between father and son, and that between friend and friend in terms of the one between elder and younger brother. . . . But these are only the major family relationships, and there were many more. In the *Erh Ya*, . . . the oldest dictionary of the Chinese language, dating from before the Christian era, there are more than one hundred terms for various family relationships, most of which have no equivalent in the English language.
>
> For the same reason ancestor worship developed. In a family living in a particular place, the ancestor worshiped was usually the first of the family who had established himself and his descendants there on the land. He thus became the symbol of the unity of the family, and such a symbol was indispensable for a large and complex organization.
>
> A great part of Confucianism is the rational justification of this social system, or its theoretical expression. Economic conditions prepared its basis, and Confucianism expressed its ethical significance.

What were these economic conditions? Of primary importance was the rural basis of three fourths or more of the total population. In China, even persons whose work brings them to the great cities, and who live there for decades, possibly for generations, still continue to regard the little rural village of their ancestors as their real "home." It is this sense of belonging, generation after generation, to one small place, that has given the Chinese family its stability and cohesiveness:

> The roots of the Chinese go deep into the earth. The carefully tilled gardens, the hand-plucked harvest, and the earthen homes all tell the story of man's intimate association with nature. On every hand a substantial peasantry industriously labors to wrest a meager livelihood from the tiny fields. Innumerable groups of farm buildings, half hidden in clumps of bamboo or willow, suggest the intensity of man's occupation of the soil, and the ever-present grave mounds serve as reminders of the heritage of this venerable land. The most significant element in the Chinese landscape is thus not the soil or vegetation or the climate, but the people. Everywhere there are human beings.[103]

[102] Fung, *A Short History of Chinese Philosophy*, p. 21.
[103] George Babcock Cressey, *China's Geographic Foundations* (New York: McGraw-Hill, 1934), p. 1. See also footnote 76 for the differing Chinese and Western conceptions of what constitutes "civilization."

Contrary to popular belief, however, the *average* Chinese family has throughout history been probably little if any larger than its Western counterpart; a widely accepted estimate puts it at five to six persons. Does this mean then that the large "joint" family of popular tradition—several generations and collateral lines all living within a single compound—was a myth? Not at all, but it does mean that it was largely an upper-class phenomenon. In the words of a leading student on the subject, Olga Lang:[104]

> It seems that in imperial China the large joint family was universally accepted as the ideal. The poor, however, were prevented from carrying it into practice mainly because the high mortality rate struck them more heavily than the well-to-do people. More of their children died; fewer adults lived to old age.

The major characteristics of the Chinese family system are well known: subordination of the individual to the group, the young to the aged, the living to the ancestors (through ancestor worship), the wife to the husband, the daughter-in-law to the mother-in-law; emphasis on progeny, not romantic love, as the prime reason for marriage, with the resulting concomitants of arranged marriage and (for the wealthy, not the poor) concubinage; intense family solidarity, giving to the individual the psychological and economic security that come through membership in a tightly knit group, but at the same time leading to frequent nepotism or parasitism.

Of the innumerable statements made both for and against the Chinese family system, we can here offer only a small sampling. In 1910 an Englishman with long administrative experience in China wrote:[105]

> Nothing is more important for an understanding of the wonderfully stable and long-lived social system of China than this fact: that the social and the political unit are one and the same, and that this unit is not the individual but the family. . . . [Thinking persons] contemplate with something like dismay the weakening or breaking of the old family bonds, which if they were sometimes a hindrance to personal advancement and had a cramping influence on the individual life, at least did much to keep within bounds the primitive instincts of selfishness and greed. . . .
>
> Most people have heard a great deal of the high standard of commercial honour that prevails among the Chinese. . . . The point to be emphasised here is that the commercial honesty of the Chinese is to a great extent dependent on and the result of their theory of the relationship between the individual and the family. . . . The Western individual who owes money and cannot or will not pay . . . may leave a stigma on his family . . . , but the debts were his own and his relations cannot be held responsible. But the identification of the interests and obligations of an individual with those of his family have in agricultural China this peculiar and socially beneficial result, that a man cannot dissolve his liabilities by such a simple process as going bankrupt or dying. His rights are inherited by his sons; so are his liabilities.

Lin Yutang, writing a quarter of a century later, regards the family with mixed feelings:[106]

---

[104] Olga Lang, *Chinese Family and Society* (New Haven, Conn.: Yale University Press, 1946), p. 16.
[105] R. F. Johnston, *Lion and Dragon in Northern China* (New York: Dutton, 1910), pp. 135-138.
[106] Lin, *op. cit.*, pp. 159, 177, 186.

Of all the rights of women, the greatest is to be a mother. . . . This, in China, has been achieved through a different conception of romance and marriage. In Chinese eyes the greatest sin of Western society is the large number of unmarried women, who, through no fault of their own . . . , are unable to express themselves (p. 152).

Where the parents are too self-centered and autocratic, it often deprives the young man of enterprise and initiative, and I consider this the most disastrous effect of the family system on Chinese character. . . . In short, the family system is the negation of individualism itself, and it holds a man back, as the reins of the jockey hold back the dashing Arabian horse (p. 177).

The respect for old age . . . is always something touching, and Professor E. A. Ross has noted that the old man in China is a most imposing figure, more dignified and good to look at than the old men in the West, who are made to feel in every way that they have passed the period of their usefulness and are now gratuitously fed by their children (p. 186).

Hu Shih warmly denies that woman's position in the family has in actual fact been nearly as low as commonly believed:[107]

The position of women in the old family was never so low as many superficial observers have led us to believe. On the contrary, woman has always been the despot of the family. . . . No other country can compete with China for the distinction of being a nation of hen-pecked husbands.

The noted sociologist Fei Hsiao-tung, however, looks at the matter from a somewhat different point of view:

It comes to be taken more or less for granted that the mother-in-law is a potential enemy of the daughter-in-law. Friction between them is taken as usual and harmony as worth special praise. Anyone who has listened to gossips among the elder women, will confirm this statement. They are never tired of cursing their daughters-in-law.

Yet he too finds certain ameliorating factors:

Disharmony in the Chia [family] should not be exaggerated. In the group, cooperation is essential. It is true that the mother-in-law has a privileged position, . . . but the educational value of her discipline should also be taken into consideration. The discipline which a boy receives from his father, a girl gets from her mother-in-law. And, as the people themselves say, in the long run justice is done; for when a girl's own son takes a wife, the mother will enjoy the same privilege as her own mother-in-law.[108]

The "group insurance" which the family provides has been stressed by another Chinese scholar:[109]

Among the concrete benefits which come to the individual from the system of filial piety is that of "group insurance." Each child . . . has his birthright, the right to . . . whatever assets the family possesses. Each aged person counts on as much comfort in his declining years as the family can possibly give. Modern Chinese have criticized this practice for its tendency to encourage weakness and dependency and for its exploitation of the younger generation by the aged. Yet

[107] Hu, *The Chinese Renaissance*, pp. 104-105.
[108] Fei Hsiao-tung, *Peasant Life in China* (New York: Dutton, 1939), pp. 48, 49-50.
[109] Han Yü-shan, "Molding Forces," in H. F. MacNair, ed., *China* (Berkeley: University of California Press, 1946), p. 7.

it has had great moral and political influence throughout the centuries in developing social fraternity and security.

John Fairbank, too, emphasizes the security that comes from belonging to a system of status:[110]

> Chinese well habituated to the family system have been prepared to accept similar patterns of status in other institutions, including the official hierarchy of the government. One advantage of a system of status (as opposed to our individualistic system of contractual relations) is that a man knows automatically where he stands in his family or society. He can have security in the knowledge that if he does his prescribed part he may expect reciprocal action from others in the system.

The sociologist Shu-ching Lee of the University of Chicago points to an important aspect of filial piety when he writes: "It is the binding force of this virtue and of its far reaching effects that has reduced juvenile delinquency to a minimum in the Chinese family." [111]

Finally, we quote several of the opinions, both favorable and unfavorable, made by Olga Lang, who has studied the Chinese family at greater length than has any of the preceding:[112]

> There are many reasons for believing that kinsmen in China were more helpful to one another than in medieval or modern Europe. We cannot point to a single European community where in a time of distress the people came to one another's aid as spontaneously as they did in Hongkong after the great fire of 1842, when, according to Legge, all the victims were tended by their kin, leaving nobody to private charity (pp. 21-22).

> Nepotism in old China reached proportions unparalleled anywhere else. Combined with overpopulation, it produced the notoriously crowded and inefficient Chinese business and government offices (p. 23).

> A wife could be repudiated by her husband on the following grounds: (1) If she disobeyed her husband's parents; (2) failed to bear children; (3) committed adultery; (4) exhibited jealousy; (5) had some repulsive disease; (6) was garrulous; (7) stole. . . . Divorce by mutual agreement, still frowned upon in Europe and America, has been recognized in China since the feudal period. . . . Husbands could not repudiate their wives for reasons other than the seven mentioned above; moreover, the ancient sages formulated "three reasons for not repudiating wives." These "three reasons" breathe a spirit of justice unsurpassed in the divorce laws of any country up to the most modern times. The wife could not be sent away (1) if she had mourned her husband's parents for three years; (2) if her husband's family had become wealthy . . . ; (3) if she had no family to take her in (pp. 40-41).

> The harsh treatment of the daughter-in-law by the mother-in-law is one of the most striking features of Chinese family life. . . . Nor should it be deduced after the fashion of some writers that China was a land of henpecked husbands. Tales of rebellious wives are more numerous simply because obedient wives were not so interesting to fiction writers: they were not "news" (pp. 48-49).

[110] Fairbank, *The United States and China*, pp. 31–32.
[111] Shu-ching Lee, "China's Traditional Family: Its Characteristics and Disintegration," *American Sociological Review*, XVIII (1953), 278.
[112] Lang, *op. cit.*, pp. 21–53, *passim*.

In old China people were not taught to expect love and happiness from marriage. Not personal satisfaction but the continuation of the family . . . was the goal of marriage. Yet certainly personal gratification was sometimes the by-product of marriage. Many couples probably enjoyed what might be called "more or less" happiness. . . . Not infrequently real affection grew up in this marriage arranged by parents (p. 49).

Polygyny was an accepted institution and a wife was not humiliated when her husband took a concubine. . . . In all circumstances the legal wife maintained her position. It was forbidden to lower one's wife to the position of a concubine or to set a concubine in her place. . . . Yet all this gives only one side of the picture. Plural marriage was far from being an idyl. . . . The stories about fights between jealous wives and concubines . . . perhaps outnumber those about wives and concubines who accept each other (pp. 50-51).

In China widows were treated less cruelly than in India—they were not burned after their husbands' deaths. But their life was miserable. The pressure of public opinion prevented them from remarrying. . . .
What mitigated the lot of Chinese women was the characteristic moderation displayed by the Chinese in interpreting all rules of behavior. Fathers, sons, and husbands often yielded to women in order to avoid disagreeable conflicts. . . . In some families women even succeeded in achieving a position of power. But this was never officially sanctioned, and in the eyes of the community women remained without rights (pp. 52-53).

Whether or not we as Westerners approve of the Chinese family system is less important than the fact that for thousands of years the Chinese themselves have accepted it, obviously because it seemed to them to meet the conditions and needs of the time. During the past half century or more, on the other hand, "modern" Chinese in increasing numbers have been attacking the family system as "feudal" or reactionary, and insisting on their right to marry and lead their family life as they please.

What has recently been happening to the family in Communist China, therefore, should be regarded less as a complete break with the past than as the universalization of a trend hitherto confined to a relatively small Western-influenced bourgeoisie. At the same time, however, the Communists have added one new element of great significance: they have emphasized that the individual's obligations to the family, formerly of overriding importance, should be supplemented by, and to some extent subordinated to, his obligations to society at large. We shall have more to say about this when we come to the question of Chinese individualism (Sect. E, 2).

Not surprisingly, evaluations of what has been recently happening often violently differ. Representative of one widespread point of view is the following statement by a political scientist—undoubtedly influenced by the many reports of mass trials and the like at which wives are said to have denounced their husbands, or children their parents: "They [the Communists] have undertaken to divide husband and wife, father and son, brothers, and friends, so far demolishing the social relationships that only the loyalty of subject to ruler remains to be exacted." [113]

[113] H. Arthur Steiner, Foreword to "Report on China," a symposium edited by himself in *Annals of the American Academy of Political and Social Science*, 277 (September, 1951), ix.

Other observers, on the other hand, while not denying that excesses have undoubtedly occurred, stress the social evils in the old (especially rural) China
which, in their opinion, made the family revolution not only inevitable but desirable. Here, for example, are the remarks of a British Quaker who remained in
China until about 1953:[114]

> I used to listen to any group discussing the past and present treatment of
> women and record their stories. Often the incidents they described were grotesque.
> A Cantonese described how he had seen women sold in a public market place,
> disposed of by their husbands to pay a debt or end a family quarrel. Some had
> been sold as many as eighteen times, and landlords would buy them, pay a per-
> centage of the purchase price to the local tax office and put them to work. A
> Fukienese recalled how men fallen in the world would take their wives to certain
> restaurants and rent them out by the night or the month. The intensity of woman's
> subjection varied from district to district.

Another observer, an American journalist, writes equally strongly of what he
saw in rural North China in 1947-1948:[115]

> In Honan Province the writer came across a landlord who had a family of
> sixty-nine members. Through this family, he controlled seven hundred tenant
> farmers, thirty slave girls, two hundred squatters and seven wet nurses who
> breast-fed his numerous brood. He was able to buy and sell women because of his
> wealth and he was also powerful because he possessed women (p. 310).

> The lowly position of Chinese women not only had a terrible effect on the
> women themselves, but also succeeded in degrading and debauching all human
> relations within society. The Chiang Kai-shek government in its twenty-year rule
> over China produced some improvement, but not much. It is true that Chiang
> Kai-shek, himself, believed in freedom of marriage and . . . that in Shanghai,
> Peiping and Hongkong there were Chinese women who had freedoms somewhat
> approaching those possessed by American women. But in the countryside, par-
> ticularly the North China countryside, the position of women was little better
> than it was fifty years ago. In fact, when you considered that the buying and sell-
> ing of women had increased in alarming proportions during the last decade, it
> was almost safe to say that the lot of Chinese women was as bad, or worse, than
> it had ever been (pp. 311-312).

The same author concludes:[116]

> It makes little difference that the Communists may be reforming the relations
> between the sexes as a means of obtaining power. Their sincerity is of no import
> at all. The fact remains they have given women a goal toward which they can
> fight. . . . No social revolution—either good or bad—ever took place without the
> existence of a great mass of disinherited people who could furnish a new group
> with a base of support. In the women of China, the Communists possessed, almost
> ready made, one of the greatest masses of disinherited human beings the world
> has ever seen. And because they found the key to the heart of these women,
> they also found one of the keys to victory over Chiang Kai-shek.

Regardless of whether one believes that the Communists have destroyed the
family, or (as is said by many Chinese other than the Communists themselves)
that they have "liberated" it, one thing seems certain: the family system, as it

[114] Peter Townsend, *China Phoenix* (London: Cape, 1955), p. 306.
[115] Jack Belden, *China Shakes the World* (New York: Harper, 1949), pp. 310, 311-312.
[116] *Ibid.*, p. 317.

once existed, is today dead. It is gone as irrevocably as the conditions which nurtured it and gave it strength.

2 Social Theory

Chinese thinking sees a close parallel between the microcosm which is the family and the macrocosm which is society at large: the relationships "natural" to the one are viewed as prototypes for the vastly more extended relationships of the other. Thus the emphasis upon status and hierarchical difference which we have seen to be characteristic of the family is equally characteristic of the greater world that lies beyond:[117]

> Society, in Chinese eyes, consists of a large number of small social units (the family, the village, the guild, etc.), each of which consists in turn of individuals varying greatly in their intellectual and physical capabilities. Because of these inequalities, it is inevitable that class differences should exist. The social order, in other words, is a rationalization of existing human inequalities.
>
> It does not follow, however, that there should be conflict between social classes. On the contrary, the welfare of the social organism as a whole depends upon harmonious co-operation among all of its units and of the individuals who comprise these units. This means that every individual, however high or low, has the obligation to perform to the best of his ability those particular functions in which he is expert and which are expected of him by society. Thus the ruler should rule benevolently, his ministers should be loyal yet at the same time ready to offer if need be their frank criticism, the farmers should produce the maximum of food, the artisans should take pride in their manufactures, the merchants should be honest in their dealings, and no one should interfere needlessly in the tasks of others for which he himself is not qualified. In other words, society should be like a magnified family, the members of which, though differing in their status and functions, all work in harmony for the common good.

Such is the Confucian theory which, implicitly or explicitly, has been recognized by all followers of that school. As early as *ca.* 300 B.C., for example, Mencius gave one of the most candid enunciations of Confucian class theory in two passages of his works:[118]

> Some labor with their brains and some labor with their brawn. Those who labor with their brains govern others; those who labor with their brawn are governed by others. Those governed by others, feed them. Those who govern others, are fed by them. This is a universal principle in the world (IIIa, 4).
>
> If there were no men of a superior grade, there would be no one to rule the countrymen. If there were no countrymen, there would be no one to support the men of superior grade (IIIa, 3).

This view of society, though originally Confucian, later came to be accepted by all schools of thought. Here, for example, is a passage which, despite its Confucian tone, was actually written by the noted Taoist Kuo Hsiang (d. A.D. 312):[119]

> Error arises when one has the qualities of a servant but is not satisfied to perform a servant's duties. Hence we may know that [the relative positions of] ruler and subject, superior and inferior, . . . conform to a natural principle of Heaven

---

[117] Bodde, "Harmony and Conflict," pp. 46-47.
[118] *Mencius*, IIIa, 3 and 4.
[119] Quoted in Fung, *A History of Chinese Philosophy*, II, 227.

and are not really caused by man. . . . Let the servants simply accept their own lot and assist each other without dissatisfaction, . . . each having his own particular duty and at the same time acting on behalf of the others. . . . Let those whom the age accounts worthy be the rulers, and those whose talents do not meet the requirements of the world be the subjects, just as Heaven is naturally high and Earth naturally low. . . . Although there is no [conscious] arrangement of them according to what is proper, the result is inevitably proper.

In another statement Kuo eloquently describes the harmony that emerges from seeming disharmony when the above principle is followed:[120]

Just as the spider and scarab, despite their humble surroundings, can spread their net or roll their ball without seeking the aid of any artisan, so for all creatures, each has that in which it is skilled. Although their skills differ, they themselves are alike in that they all practice these skills. This, then, is the kind of "skill that looks like clumsiness." Therefore the talented employer of men uses those who are skilled in squares to make squares, and those who are skilled in circles to make circles, allowing each to perform his particular skill, and thus to act in accordance with his nature. . . . That is why, being different from one another, their multitude of separate skills seem like clumsiness. Yet because everyone in the world has his own particular skill, the result seems like great skill.

We should not forget that this kind of thinking, though no longer fashionable in modern democracies, has long been current in many countries, including our own Western world. The following description of European medieval social theory, for example, though from the pen of the British economic historian R. H. Tawney, reads almost as though it had been written by a Confucian scholar:[121]

The facts of class status and inequality were rationalized in the Middle Ages by a functional theory of society. . . . Society, like the human body, is an organism composed of different members. Each member has its own function. . . . Each must receive the means suited to its station, and must claim no more. Within classes there must be equality. . . . Between classes there must be inequality. . . . Peasants must not encroach on those above them. Lords must not despoil peasants. Craftsmen and merchants must receive what will maintain them in their calling, and no more.

3 Chinese Gentry Society

According to Confucian theory, the four main classes of Chinese society were, in order of prestige, those of scholars, farmers, workers (artisans and laborers), and merchants. In this listing we have a capsulized indication of the vast gap separating Chinese traditional society from our own: scholars at the top, merchants at the bottom, and nobility, clergy, and military not even mentioned!

It is not surprising, of course, that the Confucian scholars should rank themselves at the top. In so doing, however, they were merely giving formal recognition to what for over two thousand years has been an established fact. From this enduring dominance of their own class, indeed, everything else in their equation naturally follows. Thus the reason why the scholars ranked the merchants at the bottom is that, as intellectuals (and in a manner not unknown to intellectuals elsewhere, though scarcely to the same degree), they looked down on "trade."

[120] Ibid., 220-221.
[121] R. H. Tawney, Religion and the Rise of Capitalism (London: Murray, 1926), pp. 22-23.

Likewise they excluded the nobility because, following the creation of unified empire at the end of the third century B.C., these became politically and numerically unimportant, and were replaced by a new ruling bureaucracy of scholar-officials who were salaried, appointive, nontitled, and in theory, at least, non-hereditary. As for the clergy, the reasons for their omission should be apparent from what has already been said about religion, while concerning military status we shall have more to say in a later section (D, 6).

By the first century B.C., Confucianism had become the official orthodoxy of the new empire, and under later dynasties its position was further consolidated and regularized through the system of government examinations which, held periodically throughout the empire and based primarily on the Confucian classics, eventually became *the* major avenue for entry into government service. When, in the sixteenth century, the Portuguese arrived in China, they invented the name mandarin to designate the members of this Chinese civil service (possibly, according to one theory, from the Latin *mandare,* to command, for it was indeed these men who gave the commands in China). Actually, however, the office-holders per se formed only part of a larger dominant social group—a group which further included the families and dependents of officeholders, as well as retired officeholders, holders of examination degrees who for one reason or another did not enter a political career, and—very important—rural landlords. "Gentry" is the word which in recent years has become popular as a generic designation for these various segments of China's dominant minority, the pre-eminence of which over all other social groups has today caused Chinese traditional society as a whole often to be referred to as Chinese "gentry society."

It is a seeming paradox that Confucianism, which started in the sixth century B.C., intensely concerned with preserving the institutions of a feudal and aristocratic China, should five or six centuries later succeed in becoming the official ideology of a nontitled officialdom serving a bureaucratic state. Actually, however, this development is less paradoxical than it seems; for central to Confucianism from the very beginning was an idea of key importance: that government is too vital a matter to be left solely to accidents of birth, and therefore requires that the hereditary nobles be assisted and advised in their rule by an élite body of officials who are educationally qualified for their important task. This education, furthermore, should be broadly humanistic and ethical rather than narrowly technical. Herein, of course, lies the seed which in imperial times grew into the examination system. How Confucius himself educated his disciples for government service is described as follows by H. G. Creel of the University of Chicago in his valuable book on Confucius:[122]

> He trained them with the intention of bringing about a different and, as he believed, a very much better kind of government. His objective in education was, therefore, a practical one. But it was by no means narrowly practical. Although the end of education was to bring about good government, this did not mean that the end product of education should be an efficient administrator and nothing more. Far from it, he should, in fact, be as nearly as possible the ideal man, from every point of view. He definitely should not be a mere specialist.

If we turn to the second of the social groups listed at the beginning of this section, that of the peasants, we find in their high ranking a reflection of the in-

[122] H. G. Creel, *Confucius: The Man and the Myth* (New York: John Day, 1949), p. 76.

tense concern with agriculture that has always marked the Chinese scene. How the agrarian way of life gradually expanded there during the many centuries of the feudal age—aided, according to one well-known theory, by the widespread construction of irrigation works—has been summarized as follows:[123]

> From these nuclei [centers of agricultural production in feudal China] the agrarian way of life spread outward wherever the terrain was favorable. The demonstrated ability of grain-production to support a larger population than any other occupation encouraged the use of manpower for increasingly ambitious water-control works. These enabled ever more land to be brought under cultivation, thus in turn making possible a yet greater population. Such works—built not merely for irrigation, but also, especially later, for flood control, drainage, and water transport—enabled the Chinese progressively to overcome environmental obstacles such as in the beginning would have been insuperable.
>
> At the same time, the increasing concern with agriculture caused other economic activities to decline to marginal importance. Hunting, for example, once economically significant, became the sport of the aristocracy. The pig, rather than cattle or sheep, was used as the chief food animal, because, as a scavenger, it did not require extensive land for its pasturage such as could more efficiently be devoted to crop growing. In short, the production of grain—wheat or millet in the north, and, later, rice in the south—became *the* great Chinese way of life.

The secret of the productivity of this kind of agriculture lay not only in its use of irrigation but above all in its *intensiveness:* the application of endless amounts of hand labor upon very small plots of land. As we shall see later (Sect. E, 5), the material lot of the peasant, despite his honorable status, was commonly a bitter one.

Quite the reverse was true of the merchant. Materially speaking, he was usually far better off than the peasant, yet, according to the Confucian theory, he was nothing more than a social "parasite," doing nothing productive himself but acquiring wealth through bartering the products created by others. In imperial China, with its Confucian scale of values, it was the successful government official, not the successful businessman, who represented the highest ideal, and this attitude was often concretely reinforced by government restrictions on private enterprise in the form of state monopolies and the like. The result was that, though many individually wealthy merchants existed in the old China, the mercantile class, *as a class*, never acquired power or prestige sufficient to challenge the dominance of the Confucian state. So strong, indeed, was the Confucian ethic that merchants who were well-to-do often assimilated themselves to the gentry class by giving their sons the Confucian education which, via the examinations, could lead to a government career.

The three factors we have been discussing—political dominance of the scholar-bureaucrat, economic primacy of agriculture, and inhibition of private commercial enterprise—led to a further important concomitant: the tendency of surplus capital to gravitate, not into commerce or industry, but into agricultural land. What this trend in effect meant is that the men who were scholars and officials were often at the same time either rural landlords themselves or had friends or

---

[123] D. Bodde, "Feudalism in China," in Rushton Coulborn, ed., *Feudalism in History* (Princeton, N.J.: Princeton University Press, 1956), pp. 72-73 (summarizing the theory of Owen Lattimore).

relatives who were. Here is how Owen Lattimore of the Johns Hopkins University has summed up the situation:[124]

> Grain, accumulated and stored, was beyond question the standard of real wealth in essentials. The development of money wealth in an easily invested, transferable, circulating form was weak. . . . This meant that the merchant, however wealthy, could not easily rise above the status of an agent. The landlords were the class for which he acted and the landlord, accordingly, had more power in the state than the merchant. . . . The landlords were none other than the mandarins, the "special people" who have already been mentioned—the "scholar-gentry." . . . Tax demands were pressed more lightly against the gentry and the deficiency was made up by exactions from the peasantry and from trade.

One of the best brief descriptions of this gentry class is that by Franz Michael of the University of Washington:[125]

> The gentry of imperial China were a distinct social group. They had recognized political, economic, and social privileges and powers and led a special mode of life. The gentry stood above the large mass of commoners and the so-called "mean people." They dominated the social and economic life of Chinese communities and were also the stratum from which the officials came. They were the guardians, the promoters, and representatives of an ethical system based on the tenets of Confucianism which provided the rules of society and of man's relation to man. Educated in this system, they derived from it their knowledge of the management of human affairs which was the main qualification for their leading role in Chinese society. During the later dynasties the gentry's position and qualifications became formalized. A system of examinations and degrees controlled by the government determined the membership of the gentry group, which thus came to be more easily recognized and defined. Protected by a ring of formal privileges, which relieved them from physical labor and gave them prestige and a special position in relation to the government, the gentry were all the more free to act in their dominant role.

Another illuminating analysis has been made by Wolfram Eberhard of the University of California:[126]

> The first typical characteristic of this "gentry society" which came into being in the third century B.C. and was firmly established in the first century A.D., is: no aristocracy or nobility exists. The upper and ruling class is a class whose power is based upon their socio-economic position. Therefore, in theory, it is an "open society": in theory everybody could enter its ranks. . . . The ruling class, which I call the "gentry" in order to avoid confusion with any superficially similar class in other cultures, occupied a double key-position wherein lay the secret of its power and stability. A family, belonging to the "gentry" normally had: (a) a country-home and (b) a city-home. The country-home was surrounded by the property of the family, and here lived a part of the family administering the property, i.e., collecting rent from the tenants. As soon as the family had enough capital it could afford to engage a tutor to give its children the education to become officials in town. . . .

[124] Owen Lattimore, *Inner Asian Frontiers of China* (2nd ed.; New York: American Geographical Society, 1951), pp. 47-48.
[125] Franz Michael, Introduction to Chung-li Chang, *The Chinese Gentry: Studies on Their Role in Nineteenth-Century Chinese Society* (Seattle: University of Washington Press, 1955), p. xiii.
[126] Wolfram Eberhard, *Conquerors and Rulers: Social Forces in Medieval China* (Leiden: Brill, 1952), pp. 13-16.

The educated members of our gentry family moved into the city-home. Here they could live a life of leisure: they had the solid economic background of the country-home. So we see them as poets, painters, scholars, philosophers. . . . But the normal main activity of the city-branch of the gentry-family was politics. Its members tried to enter the bureaucracy as officials in the provincial or central administration. . . .

The secret of the power and stability of this society lies in this double foothold: if in the struggle for power in the center one clique were exterminated, the country-branches of these families always could manage to survive. . . . As long as the city-branch was in power, it could protect the country-branch and assist it: the young boy from the country-branch used his city connections and secured a position. . . . If bandits or others attacked the country-seat of the family, the city-branch would give shelter to its relatives. . . . So, this gentry class was invincible. . . .

The main differences between the Western "burgher" society and this Chinese gentry society are as follows: (a) the gentry class was economically dependent upon landed property, not upon industrial capital; (b) the gentry class, comprised of landowners, scholars and politicians *in one and the same class*, normally had representatives of all three occupations *in one family*, and often one individual was at the same time scholar, politician and landlord. In the West, the scholar was always merely an appendix of the "burgher" class and usually an unhappy one; the politician and official on the other hand was normally not a landlord nor had he the highest education.

The extreme stability of Chinese gentry society was the decisive factor which prevented the disintegration of Chinese civilization and mitigated against the success of foreign rule over China. But it also prevented change. It prevented the development of modern science—the instrument of change.

4 The Confucian State

Though the gentry, as a class, dominated the Confucian state, they always remained the subjects of a hereditary ruling emperor, whose power was in theory absolute but in practice limited by several important considerations. More than a century ago an acute observer of the Chinese political scene, the British consular officer T. T. Meadows, summed up the causes for the long duration and political stability of the Chinese empire as follows:[127]

> The real causes of the unequalled duration and constant increase of the Chinese people, as one and the same nation, . . . consist of *three doctrines*, together with an *institution*. . . . The doctrines are
> I. *That the nation must be governed by moral agency in preference to physical force.*
> II. *That the services of the wisest and ablest men in the nation are indispensable to its good government.*
> III. *That the people have the right to depose a sovereign who, either from active wickedness or vicious indulgence, gives cause to oppressive and tyrannical rule.*
> The institution is
> *The system of public service competitive examinations.*

[127] Thomas Taylor Meadows, *The Chinese and Their Rebellions* (London: Smith, Elder, 1856), pp. 401-402, 403.

Concerning the merits of this examination system, Meadows writes further (p. 403):

> The institution of Public Service Examinations (which have long been strictly competitive) is *the* cause of the continued duration of the Chinese nation: it is that which preserves the other causes and gives efficacy to their operation. By it all parents throughout the country, who can compass the means, are induced to impart to their sons an intimate knowledge of the literature which contains the three doctrines above cited, together with many others conducive to a high mental cultivation. By it all the ability of the country is enlisted on the side of that Government which takes care to preserve it in purity. By it, with its impartiality, the poorest man in the country is constrained to say, that if his lot in life is a low one it is so in virtue of the "will of Heaven," and that no unjust barriers created by his fellow men prevent him from elevating himself.

Of all Chinese political institutions, none so deeply impressed foreign observers as did this system. In Europe, even in the universities, written examinations seem to have been unknown before 1702, and civil service systems based on competitive examinations did not become firmly established until the nineteenth century. Today there is considerable evidence to suggest that this innovation was inspired, at least in part, by the Chinese example, as reported by many men, notably Meadows himself.[128] We shall see in a later section (E, 3) whether Meadows' favorable view of the Chinese system was wholly justified.

Concerning Meadows' three principles, and especially the third, that of the right to depose a sovereign, he himself elaborates as follows:[129]

> The normal Chinese government is essentially based on moral force: it is not a despotism. A military and police is maintained sufficient to crush merely factious risings, but totally inadequate, both in numbers and in nature, to put down a disgusted and indignant people. But though no despotism, this same government is in form and machinery a pure autocracy. In his district the magistrate is absolute; in his province, the governor; in the empire, the Emperor. The Chinese people have no right of legislation, they have no right of self-taxation, they have not the power of voting out their rulers or of limiting or stopping supplies. *They have therefore the right of rebellion.* Rebellion is in China the old, often exercised, legitimate, and constitutional means of stopping arbitrary and vicious legislation and administration.

This theory, known in Chinese as that of T'ien Ming, "the Mandate of Heaven," is among the most ancient, for it goes back to the second millennium B.C. In essence, it asserts that as long as a sovereign rules well, he enjoys the Mandate or approval of Heaven, but, should he rule badly, he thereby forfeits the Mandate, and it then becomes legitimate for the people to overthrow him and establish another sovereign in his place. The distinction between this theory and the European one of the Divine Right of Kings is worth noting:

> The vital feature distinguishing this T'ien Ming theory from superficially similar theories elsewhere, such as that of the Divine Right of Kings, is the Chinese insistence on the fact that Heaven may conceivably transfer the Mandate from one ruling house to another. That is to say, even after Heaven has once conferred its

---

[128] See Ssu-yü Teng, "Chinese Influence on the Western Examination System," *Harvard Journal of Asiatic Studies,* VII (1943), 267-312; summarized in Teng, "China's Examination System and the West," in MacNair, ed., *op. cit.,* pp. 441-451.
[129] Meadows, *op. cit.,* pp. 23-24.

Mandate on a certain ruling house, it may thereafter withdraw it at any time, should that house prove to be unworthy. This distinction is important, because it means that in ancient China, unlike some other early civilizations, the king was definitely not regarded as a divine being. On the contrary, he was a man like other men, though one who, because of his superior qualities, had been chosen by Heaven to carry out its divine purpose. This explains why in later times [in post-feudal China] the theory was repeatedly invoked to justify the numerous changes of dynasty that have taken place in China, and why even today the Chinese term for revolution is *ko ming*, which literally means "transferring the Mandate." [130]

We have already seen (Sect. C, 3) that one of the emperor's primary functions was to maintain harmony between the human and natural worlds, and that untoward natural phenomena of all kinds were therefore interpreted as indications that something had gone wrong in human society. This theory merged with that of the Mandate of Heaven to provide the Confucian officials with a potent instrument for criticizing the throne or the administration. Such criticism we know they often made. Indeed, there is evidence suggesting that sometimes, when they lacked the actual phenomena for pointing up their criticism, they may even have fabricated false reports of such phenomena for this purpose.[131]

The heavy burden of moral responsibility which these and other aspects of Confucian political philosophy placed upon the Chinese ruler is indicated by the long series of penitential edicts dating all the way from the late second millennium B.C. to the beginning of the present century. A good modern example is the edict of August 22, 1862, issued in the name of the youthful emperor of that time by the two coregent empresses dowager:[132]

> During the night of the fifteenth of the seventh month, a flight of many shooting stars was suddenly seen moving toward the southwest; on the nights of the twenty-sixth and twenty-seventh, a comet appeared twice in the northwest. That Supreme Blue One [Heaven], when thus sending down its manifestations, does not produce such portents in vain. Moreover, beginning last month and continuing without abatement until now, an epidemic has been rife in the capital. Truly, though we be of tender years, we are filled with deepest dread and apprehension. By the Empresses Dowager we have been instructed that these warnings, transmitted by Heaven to man, are surely indicative of present deficiencies in our conduct of government. . . .

We should not end this section without quoting the very important distinction made by Meadows between "revolution" and "rebellion" in China:

> Revolution is a change of the form of government and of the principles on which it rests: it does not necessarily imply a change of rulers. Rebellion is a rising against the rulers which, far from necessarily aiming at a change of government principles and forms, often originates in a desire of preserving them intact. Revolutionary movements are against principles; rebellions against men. . . . Bearing the above distinction in mind, great light may be thrown by one sentence over 4,000 years of Chinese history: *Of all nations that have attained a certain degree of civilization, the Chinese are the least revolutionary and the most rebellious.*

[130] Bodde, "Authority and Law in Ancient China," p. 49.
[131] See Hans Bielenstein, "An Interpretation of the Portents in the Ts'ien Han Shu," *Bulletin of the Museum of Far Eastern Antiquities*, No. 22 (Stockholm, 1950), pp. 127-143.
[132] Cited in Bodde, "Authority and Law in Ancient China," p. 50, note 8.

Speaking generally, there has been but one great political revolution in China, when the centralized form of government was substituted for the feudal, about 2,000 years ago.[133]

5 Law

Confucian political theory emphasized moral and intellectual attainments as prerequisites for good government, preferred suasive to compulsive measures, and viewed the conduct of the state in terms of interpersonal relationships rather than depersonalized administrative machinery. At the same time it saw the world of man as a reflection of the natural order. All these factors combined in China to make the law subsidiary to flexibly interpreted custom and moral tradition— what we in the West would call "natural law." Here is the way the late Jean Escarra, a leading French jurist, has summed up the situation:[134]

> In the West the law has always been revered as something more or less sacrosanct, the queen of gods and men, imposing itself on everyone like a categorical imperative, defining and regulating, in an abstract way, the effects and conditions of all social activity. . . . But as one passes to the East, this picture fades away. At the other end of Asia, China has felt able to give to law and jurisprudence but an inferior place in that powerful body of spiritual and moral values which she has created. . . . Though not without juridical institutions, she has been willing to recognise only the natural order, and to exalt only the rules of morality. . . . The State and its delegate the judge have always seen their power restricted in face of the omnipotence of the heads of clans and guilds, the fathers of families, and the general administrators, who laid down the duties of each individual in his respective domain, and settled all conflicts according to equity, usage, and local custom.

In the opinion of Shu-ching Lee, this Chinese attitude derives especially from the central position held by the family in Confucian thinking: "In so far as the government was nothing but a projection of the patriarchal family, and the virtue which justified the sovereign's holding of the throne was a projected family ethics, there could never be a government of laws as practised in the West, but a government of men." [135] This means, of course, that we cannot expect to find in China that regard for "due process" which is such a cornerstone of Western juridical thinking. Thus we are told further by Escarra:[136]

> In this [Chinese] conception, there is no place for law in the Latin sense of the term. Not even rights of individuals are guaranteed by law. There are only duties and mutual compromises governed by the ideas of order, responsibility, hierarchy and harmony. The prince, assisted by the sages, ensures the dominance of these throughout the realm.

---

[133] Meadows, *op. cit.*, p. 25. Had Meadows been writing today, he would indubitably have recognized the movements convulsing China during the century since his time as constituting a second major revolution.

[134] Jean Escarra, *Le droit chinois* (Peiping: Henri Vetch, 1936), p. 3; trans. in Joseph Needham, *op. cit.*, II, 521.

[135] Shu-ching Lee, "Administration and Bureaucracy: The Power Structure in Chinese Society," *Transactions of the Second World Congress of Sociology* (London: International Sociological Association, 1954), II, 4.

[136] Escarra, *op. cit.*, p. 17; trans. in Needham, *op. cit.*, II, 529.

In its concrete provisions, Chinese law was, until the nineteenth century, in many respects more humane than that of Western Europe.[137] As pointed out by Duyvendak, however, its underlying *spirit* made it ill adapted to the needs of a modern state:[138]

> Law can never be complete and should be supplemented by the standards which live in the people. This last truth, so long forgotten in the western conception of law, when the *Juristenrecht* prevailed, has always been alive in China. It has led to the other extreme of making law but a reflex of natural, customary law, without any regularizing force of its own. . . . Government measures are therefore obeyed, in so far as they correspond with this popular sense of rightness, not merely because it is positive law. Therefore innovations, which are not consecrated by custom, are ignored. This is one of the great problems which modern China has to face. In a modern state, with highly complicated economical and social conditions, the old conception of law is ill-fitted.

There is no doubt that the differing Chinese and Western legal conceptions have led to much friction ever since the early nineteenth century and have been repeatedly invoked by the Western powers as justification for extracting extraterritoriality, foreign concessions, and like privileges from China. These in turn have generated strong Chinese resentments, the effects of which are still seen in the intense nationalism found in China today.

6 Militarism

The reasons for excluding the military from the recognized Confucian social hierarchy should by now be obvious. In the words of John Fairbank:[139]

> The standard dogma perpetuated by Chinese scholars and civilian chroniclers has been that "good iron is not used to make a nail nor a good man to make a soldier." This expresses the idea of the literatus who governs by moral sanctions and uses every opportunity to disparage the warrior who takes power by force.

The question arises, however: Was this dogma of the Confucianists generally shared by other segments of society? The overwhelming opinion of observers is that it was. As long ago as the seventeenth century, for example, Matteo Ricci wrote that "fighting and violence among the people are practically unheard of. . . . On the contrary, one who will not fight and restrains himself from returning a blow is praised for his prudence and bravery." [140] And as recently as 1949 an American sociologist wrote in similar vein:[141]

> Soldiers have for centuries been considered the lowest rung of Chinese society. The present Chinese government has been at some pains to change this conception, as have the Chinese Communist groups. The latter seem to have had the more success along these lines, but by and large the Chinese still aver that "good iron is not used for nails; good men do not become soldiers."

Still more recently, however, another American sociologist, Morton Fried of Columbia, has taken strong exception to this view. Unfortunately, space permits

---

[137] See above, Sect. A, 2, near end.
[138] J. J. L. Duyvendak, *The Book of Lord Shang* (London: Probsthain, 1928), pp. 129–130.
[139] Fairbank, *The United States and China*, p. 50.
[140] See Sect. A, 2. See also Marco Polo's similar opinion, there cited.
[141] Marion J. Levy, *The Family Revolution in Modern China* (Cambridge, Mass.: Harvard University Press, 1949), p. 49, note.

us to quote only excerpts from his conclusions and not from his detailed arguments themselves:[142]

> We have alluded to a mass of historical, biographical, and sociological data which reveals that military status, far from being low or despised, has frequently enjoyed the highest rating. This version of the position of military personnel is more in accord with the facts of Chinese culture, agreeing with such normally inconsistent factors as the frequent preoccupation with war and rebellion, the prominence of military events and characters in art and literature, and the importance of military supernaturals in the pantheon. Applied to contemporary affairs, it necessitates a re-evaluation of the often conjectured sudden rise of militarism in China, which is seen as a diffusion from the West. . . .
>
> It should be emphasized that neither military nor civil status has been unconditionally ascendant during the past two millenniums in China's history. The two have been related in various ways; at times competing with one or the other dominant, at times harmoniously interacting.

Against this view a third sociologist, this time Chinese, has written a rebuttal from which, again, we can cite only excerpts:[143]

> Military status in Chinese history may have been higher and lower as situations changed; a threatening barbarian invasion, for instance, might enhance the prestige of the military. . . . And the chaos of civil strife might also place a number of military generals in high civil posts. But these facts do not warrant a generalization that the military has always enjoyed a status higher than, or even equal to, that of the literati. . . .
>
> In a sound sociological study of military status in China, the author has to tackle effectively the following problems . . . : (1) Who constitute the soldiery? It is a well-established fact that the literati are mainly recruited from the landowning gentry, whereas the military, especially the mercenaries, [come] from the poor and illiterate peasantry, and, therefore, the former hold a higher status. (2) What is the general behavior of an ordinary soldier? If he behaved not otherwise than as described in the popular song cited by the author . . . [in which a soldier boasts that with his gun he can seize anything he wants] . . . , he cannot but be despised. (3) What is the psychological orientation of the common people toward the military and literati? Would a peasant prefer to see his son go to school for study or join the army for drill, if he could afford to do either? He would probably choose the former.

Nevertheless, factors do exist, both historical and sociological, which at first sight lend color to Fried's thesis. Thus on the historical side, Fairbank is only stating a well-known fact when he remarks that, despite the weight of Confucian tradition,

> . . . few empires in history have had a more impressive military record. In periods of strong government . . . powerful military expeditions have gone beyond China's borders. . . . Meanwhile every dynasty has been founded by the sword. Decades at a time have seen an endless succession of rebel hordes, imperial armies, and alien invaders marching across the face of the land.[144]

---

[142] Morton Fried, "Military Status in Chinese Society," *American Journal of Sociology*, LVII (1952), 355.
[143] Shu-ching Lee, "Comment" on foregoing, *ibid.*, pp. 356–357.
[144] Fairbank, *The United States and China*, p. 50

Sociologically speaking, too,

> . . . it is also true that many of the most popular Chinese novels and dramas—from which, until recently, the ordinary man derived much of his knowledge of Chinese history—deal in most colorful fashion with famous wars and military figures of the past. . . . Another factor of some sociological importance is that many of China's historical military heroes began their careers as bandits and have become identified in the popular mind as Robin Hood-like protagonists of the people against a corrupt social order.[145]

Before reaching conclusions, however, we should read Professor Fairbank's further remarks on the nature of the Chinese military tradition:[146]

> The Chinese military tradition is of a different type from the European or the Japanese. Once an imperial regime has been instituted, civilian government has been esteemed over military. It took a soldier to found a dynasty but he and his descendants invariably found it easier to rule as sages, through civilian officials. . . . Chinese history has had no counterpart to the Elizabethan or Japanese institutions of maritime adventure and piracy whereby the central power waxed strong on its overseas takings. No doubt one factor was the early disappearance of feudalism.

Unquestionably, too, it has often happened, particularly in times of economic pressure or political disorder, that peasants have been obliged to abandon their land and become soldiers or bandits (between which, at such times, there was often little difference). This fact, however, by no means proves that they had any real preference for these two occupations. Rather, it reflects the obvious truth that in a society lacking a well-developed industrial and commercial economy the peasant was left with scarcely any other real alternatives.

As an eyewitness of the Communist triumph in China in 1949, this writer had ample opportunity to observe the high esteem enjoyed by the soldiers of the Red armies, and to compare it with the fear, dislike, or contempt only too commonly accorded the Chinese soldier in the past. On the basis of what he has seen, it is hard for him to believe that the present attitude represents nothing new in Chinese history.

7 The Ruler of "All-under-Heaven"

A major cause of friction between China and the West, especially in the nineteenth century, was the traditional Chinese attitude toward the world beyond their borders—an attitude stemming both from historico-geographic and ideological factors. In what follows we base ourselves largely on John Fairbank's excellent study on this subject:[147]

> Ever since the bronze age, when the civilization of the Shang dynasty (*ca.* 1500-1100 B.C.) had first appeared as a culture-island in the Yellow River basin, the inhabitants of the Chinese state had been surrounded by barbarian peoples of inferior culture. At no time were they in direct contact with an equal civilization, for all of Eastern Asia—Korea, Japan, Annam, Siam—became culturally

---

[145] Bodde, "Harmony and Conflict," p. 54.
[146] Fairbank, *The United States and China*, pp. 50–51.
[147] Fairbank, "Tributary Trade and China's Relations with the West," 129–134, *passim.*

affiliated to the Middle Kingdom, while India and the Near East remained cut off by the arid land mass of Central Asia. . . .

From this age-old contact with the barbarians roundabout, . . . the Chinese were impressed with one fact: that their superiority was not one of mere material power but of culture. . . . So great was their virtue, so overwhelming the achievements of the Middle Kingdom in art and letters and the art of living, that no barbarian could long resist them. Gradually but invariably the barbarian in contact with China tended to become Chinese, by this most flattering act reinforcing the Chinese conviction of superiority. . . . After centuries of solitary grandeur as the center of Eastern Asia, the Chinese developed what may be called, by analogy to nationalism, a spirit of "culturism." Those who did not follow the Chinese way were *ipso facto* inferior (pp. 129-130).

[According to Confucianism] there was felt to be a certain virtue or power in right conduct such that it could move others. The virtuous ruler—that is, the one who did the right thing—merely by being virtuous gained prestige and influence over people. . . . By a logical expansion of this theory the emperor's virtuous action was believed to attract irresistibly the barbarians who were outside the pale of Chinese civilization proper. . . .

Thus the relationship between the emperor and the barbarians came to symbolize the actual historical relationship between China as the center of culture and the rude tribes roundabout. This relationship was clearly recognized and formed the theoretical basis for the tributary system. The first tenet of this theory —and this is an interpretation—was that the uncultivated alien, however crass and stupid, could not but appreciate the superiority of Chinese civilization and would naturally seek to "come and be transformed" (*lai-hua*) and so participate in its benefits. To do this it was chiefly essential that he should recognize the unique position of the Son of Heaven. . . .

Secondly, the relationship which thus inhered between the outer barbarian and the emperor was by no means unilateral and indeed could hardly exist except on a reciprocal basis. It was the function of the emperor to be compassionate and generous. His "tender cherishing of men from afar" (*huai-jou yuan-jen*) is one of the clichés in all documents on foreign relations. . . .

Finally, it was unavoidable that these reciprocal relations of compassionate benevolence and humble submission should be carried out in ritual form. . . . Tribute thus became one of the rites of the Court, a part of the ceremonial of government. . . . Its presentation by the barbarians was a sign of their admission to the civilization of the Middle Kingdom—a boon and a privilege, not an ignominious ordeal. The formalities of the tributary system constituted a mechanism by which formerly barbarous regions outside the empire were given their place in the all-embracing Sinocentric cosmos (pp. 132-133).

In this tributary system, it was the symbolic significance of the tribute objects, not their material value, that counted:

The tribute itself was no gain to the imperial court. It was supposed to consist of native produce, a symbolic offering of the fruits of the tributary country. . . . The value of the tribute objects was certainly balanced, if not outweighed, by the imperial gifts to the various members of the mission and to the vassal ruler.[148]

How this symbolic significance was expressed in the ritual act of tribute presentation is vividly described by Fairbank as follows:

[148] *Ibid.*, p. 135.

The tribute mission was entertained at banquets, not once but several times, and banqueted also in the presence of the emperor. . . . On their part the tributary envoys performed the kotow. . . . The kotow in principle is a knocking of the head upon the ground, in itself an act of surrender, but the full kotow as performed at court was a good deal more. It consisted of three separate kneelings, each kneeling accompanied by three separate prostrations, and the whole performed at the strident command of a lowly usher—"Kneel!," "Fall prostrate!," "Rise to your knees!," "Fall prostrate!," and so on. An envoy went through this calisthenic ceremony not once but many times. . . . It was the rite above all others which left no doubt, least of all in the mind of the performer, as to who was the superior and who the inferior in status (p. 134).

For centuries this ceremony was periodically performed by envoys from kingdoms and peoples scattered across the face of Asia—including, at certain periods, even such remote places as Aden and the Somali coast of East Africa. With the coming of the Europeans to China, the system was automatically applied to them as well: between 1655 and 1795 some seventeen missions were received at the Chinese court from Russia, Portugal, Holland, the Papacy, and Britain, of which all but that of 1793 from Britain appear to have performed the kotow.

Nowhere is Chinese ethnocentrism better exemplified than in the letter written by the Emperor of China to King George III as a result of this last mission. Possibly its tone was heightened by the fact that on this occasion the British envoy, Lord Macartney, wholly refused to kotow and agreed instead only to kneel upon one knee before the Chinese monarch:[149]

You, O King, live beyond the confines of many seas, nevertheless, impelled by your humble desire to partake of the benefits of our civilisation, you have dispatched a mission respectfully bearing your memorial. . . . I have perused your memorial: the earnest terms in which it is couched reveal a respectful humility on your part, which is highly praiseworthy. In consideration of the fact that your Ambassador and his deputy have come a long way with your memorial and tribute, I have shown them high favour and have allowed them to be introduced into my presence. . . .

As to your entreaty to send one of your nationals to be accredited to my Celestial Court . . . , this request is contrary to all usage of my dynasty and cannot possibly be entertained. . . . Supposing that your Envoy should come to our Court, his language and national dress differ from that of our people, and there would be no place in which to bestow him. . . . Besides, supposing I sent an Ambassador to reside in your country, how could you possibly make for him the requisite arrangements? Europe consists of many other nations besides your own: if each and all demanded to be represented at our Court, how could we possibly consent? . . .

Swaying the wide world, I have but one aim in view, namely, to maintain a perfect governance and to fulfil the duties of the State: strange and costly objects do not interest me. If I have commanded that the tribute offerings sent by you, O King, are to be accepted, this was solely in consideration for the spirit which prompted you to dispatch them from afar. Our dynasty's majestic virtue has penetrated unto every country under Heaven, and Kings of all nations have offered their costly tribute by land and sea. As your Ambassador can see for himself, we possess all things. I set no value on objects strange or ingenious, and

[149] Several translations of this famous letter are available. The one followed here is that of E. Backhouse and J. O. P. Bland, *Annals and Memoirs of the Court of Peking* (Boston: Houghton Mifflin, 1914), pp. 322-325. By courtesy of the publishers.

have no use for your country's manufactures. This then is my answer to your request to appoint a representative at my Court. . . . It behoves you, O King, to respect my sentiments and to display even greater devotion and loyalty in future, so that, by perpetual submission to our Throne, you may secure peace and prosperity for your country hereafter. . . . A special mandate.

Less than fifty years later China's "glorious isolation" was smashed by the Anglo-Chinese war of 1839-1842 (commonly known as the Opium War), and with this event the Confucian cosmos epitomized by this letter began to crumble. During the next century China suffered repeated humiliations from the West— many of them unfortunately well calculated to confirm her traditional opinion regarding the "barbarian" peoples beyond her borders. Such is the background of ideas and events that should be pondered when examining the surging nationalism today so evident in China, as in many other parts of Asia.

E. DEMOCRACY, THE INDIVIDUAL, AND SOCIAL MOBILITY [150]

1 Democracy in China

In 1949, just when the government of Chiang Kai-shek was making its last stand against the Communists on the Chinese mainland, the United States Department of State issued a famous "White Paper" on China in which Dean Acheson, then Secretary of State, expressed the following hope: "We continue to believe that . . . ultimately the profound civilization and the democratic individualism of China will reassert themselves and she will throw off the foreign yoke." [151]

Was this hope justified, and is it appropriate to apply terms like "democracy" or "individualism" to China? On these and similar questions there rages much controversy, from which we have space here to quote only a very few representative opinions.

Many scholars (as well as others who are not scholars) have used "democracy" to describe the tenets of Confucianism, and especially of its major ancient protagonists, Confucius himself and Mencius. It is undoubtedly these two men, for example, that Dr. Hu Shih primarily had in mind when he wrote: "The classical age was one of mental freedom and independence, an age of democratic ideas." Or again: "It has become a tradition for scholars to fight against tyrannical monarchs and corrupt officials in the interests of the state and the people. From this stems China's fight for freedom and democracy through the ages. The democratic tradition has developed primarily from Confucianism." [152]

Likewise Professor Creel has this to say about Confucius himself: [153]

> Not every thinker who has approved of democracy as an abstract principle has been able to provide for it a consistent philosophy fulfilling its rather difficult requirements. The philosophy of Confucius did this to an unusual degree. . . . To say that the philosophy of Confucius was democratic in the full modern sense of that term would be going too far. On the other hand, it does not go too far to say that Confucius was a forerunner of democracy. . . . He provided for democracy not merely a philosophy but a battle cry. Still more remarkable, he was able . . . to call for sacrifice in the name of the democratic cause without ever making excessive claims. . . . It [the body of ideals advocated by Confucius] resembled what is today called the "democratic way of life," except that Confucius advocated it with more zeal and enthusiasm than is often associated with modern democracy.

Many people, however, regard Mencius, perhaps even more than Confucius, as *the* great exponent of ancient Chinese democracy on two main counts: (1) He,

---

[150] Strictly speaking, these topics belong to the preceding section, but because of their length and importance it is more convenient to treat them here separately.
[151] *United States Relations with China; with Special Reference to the Period 1944-1949* (Washington: Government Printing Office, 1949), p. xvi.
[152] Hu Shih, "Chinese Thought," in MacNair, ed., *op. cit.*, pp. 223, 224.
[153] Creel, *Confucius*, pp. 288-289.

more than any other Confucian, elaborated the ancient theory of the Mandate of Heaven—the so-called "right of rebellion"—and made it an accepted part of Confucian doctrine. It is Mencius, for example, who flatly asserted that "the people are the most important element" in a state, whereas the sovereign is the least. (2) Likewise it is Mencius who exalted the moral worth of the individual by asserting that all men without exception are born good and therefore may achieve sagehood if they will but cultivate the shoots of goodness that are present at birth. "All men," he said, "may become a Yao or a Shun [legendary sage-rulers]." [154] This belief in universal perfectibility, with its implicit rejection of predestination or original sin, has for more than eight centuries been *the* unquestioned axiom of Chinese thinking. It is one of several reasons why the spread of Christianity in China—at least in certain of its forms—has proved difficult.

Yet there are contradictions in Confucianism too. Thus it is Confucius who says, "With education, [there is] no class." But it is also Confucius who says, "The people can be made to follow it [probably meaning a policy decreed from above]; they cannot be made to understand it." [155] Likewise, it is Mencius who says that all men can become sages, yet it is also Mencius who accepts the social division between the brain workers who govern the brawn workers, and the brawn workers who feed the brain workers, as "a universal principle in the world." [156]

Here we find a dichotomy that is characteristic of Confucianism: socially it is democratic inasmuch as it grants to all men the possibility of moral and intellectual improvement, yet politically it is paternalistic inasmuch as it reserves governmental activity to a moral and educational élite, while denying it to the people at large. In other words, Confucianism sanctifies a structured and highly hierarchical society, yet at the same time grants to individuals the possibility of moving upward or downward within this social structure. This point should become clearer as we progress further.

2 Chinese Individualism

Is there such a thing as "individualism" in China? Here again it is easy to find arguments on both sides. On the negative side, the following are a few of many indications that could be cited: The Westerner asserts his ego by placing his personal name first, then his family name (John SMITH, not SMITH John). The Chinese (unless, as in the case of many of those cited in this book, he is writing for Westerners) does just the reverse (SUN Yat-sen, not Yat-sen SUN). The Westerner unthinkingly speaks and writes in terms of "I" and "you." The Chinese (in the past, much less now) tended to avoid such direct address by using instead indirect locutions in the third person, such as "humble person" (referring to the self), and "sir" or "gentleman" (referring to the other person). In the West, words like "individual" or "democracy" have had a long history, whereas in China no real linguistic equivalents existed until, in recent times, coined terms were deliberately invented. In short, it could be argued that Chinese thinking has tra-

---

[154] *Mencius,* VIIb, 14, and VIb, 2, respectively.
[155] *Analects* of Confucius, XV, 38, and VIII, 9, respectively.
[156] See Sect. D, 2.

ditionally subordinated the individual to the group (Confucianism), the human group to Nature (Taoism), or has even completely denied the existence of an enduring self or ego (Buddhism). Speaking of the social sphere, Francis Hsu contrasts the Chinese and American (he could equally well say Western) views of the individual as follows:[157]

> In the American way of life the emphasis is placed upon the predilections of the individual, a characteristic we shall call *individual-centered*. This is in contrast to the emphasis the Chinese put upon an individual's appropriate place and behavior among his fellowmen, a characteristic we shall term *situation-centered*. . . . Being individual-centered, the American moves toward social and psychological isolation. . . . Being more situation-centered, the Chinese is inclined to be socially or psychologically dependent on others.

If we turn to the other side of the argument, however, we can find in Confucianism a conception of personality which possibly merits the term "individualism," provided we are willing to stretch its usual connotations. Its marks are an innate personal dignity, a pride in work, and a sense of decorum toward others, which can be found in the humblest peasant, and are known to anyone who has lived closely with the Chinese.

Basic to this Confucian concept of personality are two postulates to which we have already referred: the moral worth of every individual and the fact that he is above all a *social* being, that is, a being living in a context of social relationships wherein he holds fixed status as well as fixed responsibilities. Confucian "individualism," therefore, means the fullest development by the individual of his creative potentialities—not, however, merely for the sake of self-expression but because he can thus best fulfill that particular role which is his within his social nexus. "Individuation"—a term borrowed from the psychologists—is very possibly a better word than "individualism" to describe this distinctive ideal. Here, for example, is the way the psychologist Jung distinguishes between the two words:[158]

> Individualism consists in deliberately giving prominence to and emphasizing presumed originality, as opposed to collective considerations and responsibilities. Individuation on the other hand means a better and more complete fulfilment of man's collective responsibilities, in that, by making adequate allowance for what is peculiar to an individual, better fulfilment of his social aptitudes may be expected than when these characteristics are neglected or suppressed. . . . Individuation can therefore only represent a process of psychological development leading to the fulfilment of given individual conditions or, in other words, to the evolution of the particular predetermined entity that is man as we know him. He does not thereby become "selfish" in the generally accepted sense of the term, but simply fulfils his own specific nature. As we have already noted, there is a world of difference between this and egoism or individualism.

Dr. Abegg, after quoting this passage, goes on to apply it to what she sees as characteristic of China (as well as other parts of East Asia):[159]

> This concept of individuation coincides exactly with the basic outlook of the East Asians. It provides the explanation for the fact that the East Asians are

[157] Hsu, *op. cit.*, p. 10.
[158] Carl G. Jung, as quoted in Lily Abegg, *The Mind of East Asia* (New York: Thames & Hudson, 1952), p. 186.
[159] Abegg, *op. cit.*, pp. 186-187.

deeply conscious that the point at issue is not so much the realization of an individual being (in our sense!) as of a given human type. Since, according to the organic view of things, every man has his own particular place in society, with which a special "way" (Tao) is associated, it follows that the process of individuation can only be accomplished in conformity with this "way." The East Asian strives to become the perfect type of craftsman or artist, of learned man or soldier, and by achieving this aim he becomes at the same time a perfect being—a "personality."

Diametrically opposed to this Confucian concept of the individual, there is another interpretation of "individualism" which is widely current in China today, and one in which the word becomes a synonym for uncontrolled self-seeking, license, and utter indifference to public welfare. Against such anarchistic individualism (as well as "liberty," with which it is often linked) many Chinese reformers and intellectuals have powerfully inveighed. Here, for example, is what Sun Yat-sen said in 1924:[160]

> Why has China become a sheet of loose sand? Simply because of excessive individual liberty. Therefore the aims of the Chinese Revolution are different from the aims in foreign revolutions, and the methods we use must also be different. . . . Europeans rebelled and fought because they had too little liberty. But we, because we have had too much liberty without any unity and resisting power, because we have become a sheet of loose sand and so have been invaded by foreign imperialism, . . . must break down individual liberty and become pressed together into an unyielding body like the firm rock which is formed by the addition of cement to sand.

Writing some ten years later, Lin Yutang correctly attributed this destructive form of individualism to the overriding dominance of the family above all other social concerns (a perversion, as we have seen, of the true teachings of Confucianism):[161]

> The Chinese are a nation of individualists. They are family-minded, not social-minded, and the family mind is only a form of magnified selfishness. . . . "Public spirit" is a new term, so is "civic consciousness," and so is "social service." There are no such commodities in China (p. 172).

> The family, with its friends, became a walled castle, with the greatest communistic cooperation and mutual help within, but coldly indifferent toward, and fortified against, the world without. In the end, as it worked out, the family became a walled castle outside which everything is legitimate loot (p. 180).

These and many similar statements, made by prominent non-Communists decades ago, show that the present-day attacks on "individualism" should by no means be attributed solely to Marxism; they also represent intensified reactions to what has long been felt as a very serious weakness in Chinese society. As such, they are germane to the present-day thinking about the family which we have discussed earlier.

At the same time it is worth noting that when, as constantly happens in China today, the Communist authorities appeal to the people for what might be called "self-expression through social service" (though this is not their actual termi-

---

[160] Sun Yat-sen, *San Min Chu I: The Three Principles of the People,* trans. Frank W. Price (6th. ptg.; Shanghai: The Commercial Press, 1930), p. 210.
[161] Lin, *op. cit.,* pp. 172, 180.

nology), they are in effect reinforcing and adapting to a new milieu the other age-old Confucian ideal of the individual which we have termed "individuation." And finally, it should be noted that neither this nor the self-seeking individualism which is so strongly attacked really coincides to any great extent with Western classical definitions of the word, as found, for example, in John Stuart Mill's famous essay *On Liberty*.

3 Social Mobility: The Examination System

Let us turn now from ideology to the concrete and important problem of social mobility in the old China: To what extent was movement between social classes actually possible? Of all institutions making such movement at least theoretically possible there is no doubt that the examination system was by far the most important. We have already seen (Sect. D, 4) how more than a century ago Meadows hailed this system as *the* major cause for the long duration and stability of Chinese civilization. Among the innumerable writers who have expressed similar opinions, we shall again, as when discussing Chinese democracy, take Hu Shih and H. G. Creel as good Chinese and Western representatives. On the Chinese side, Dr. Hu tells us:[162]

> Confucius had laid down a democratic educational philosophy in four words: "With education, [there is] no class." This germinal idea was worked out in the civil service examination system, which was competitive, objective, and open to practically everyone of ability. It broke down class distinctions, feudalism, and artificial barriers of race, tribe, religion, and color. Prior to its abolition in 1905 it was China's most effective tool in the fight for political equality.

Similarly, we are told by Professor Creel:[163]

> Despite its shortcomings, the examination system gave China a unique kind of government which had many advantages. It brought many of the ablest men in the country into government service. In so far as it was effective, it assured that officials were men of culture, not mere wasters who had inherited their position. Because its very basis was the philosophy and the ethics of Confucianism, it inculcated a body of shared ideals which produced a very unusual *esprit de corps*. Although it fell short of what we today consider political democracy, it gave to the common people a kind of representation in the government, since in each generation some of their number won official posts. It did not make a classless society since education automatically raised the status of its possessors, but it did bring about a degree of social democracy that has probably never been equalled in so great a country over such a long period. Where every peasant's son may in theory hope to become the most powerful minister in the government, and one of their number does occasionally reach such a position, a certain limit is set to social stratification.

In recent years, however, there has been a growing tendency to question the traditional interpretation and to see in the examinations an ingenious instrument which, despite its avowedly egalitarian aim, served in actual fact to retain political power very largely within an exclusive ruling group. The following are representative examples of this viewpoint:

[162] Hu, "Chinese Thought," p. 226.
[163] Creel, *Confucius*, pp. 252-253.

This system has been praised as an institution which, by its general accessibility, gave Chinese society its democratic character, its flexibility, durability and wisdom. Does this statement hold true? . . . A final study has still to be made, but our preliminary analysis seems to confirm absolutely what the qualitative investigation by Chinese scholars had previously indicated. Some "fresh blood" may have been absorbed from the lower strata of society by means of the examination system; but on the whole the ruling officialdom reproduced itself socially more or less from its own ranks. The Chinese system of examinations had a very definite function; but, as in the case of the family, this function is by no means what popular legend has thus far made us believe it was.[164]

Literacy was the link that made the scholar-gentry-landlord mandarins a ruling class of Siamese twins: a recondite literacy, which fostered difficulty and mystery in the written language and consciously resisted simplification and wide dissemination among the people. It "separated social classes but united regions." It required a long apprenticeship, which could only be afforded by families of leisure, so that the nominal equality of all men in the public examination halls was in fact an equality of opportunity only for those who already monopolized the power of the state.[165]

The most detailed indictment of the examination system, however, is that of the sociologist Chung-li Chang of the University of Washington, which is based on his comprehensive study of its operation during the nineteenth century:[166]

It has been said that the examination system lasted for more than a thousand years because of its "spirit of equality." In theory, the way was open for any commoner to rise to gentry status and official position. The examination system did indeed make possible a certain "equality of opportunity," but the advantages were heavily in favor of those who had wealth and influence.

One social group was entirely excluded. Members of families of slaves, servants, prostitutes, entertainers, lictors, and others classified among the "mean people" were forbidden to participate in the examinations.

Many exceptions to the principle of equality can also be seen within the examination system. For instance, *chü-jen* degrees or official positions were sometimes granted to sons or grandsons of high officials, to those who detected and reported rebellious activities, or to those who contributed to the military fund or were active in relief work. Some could thus obtain degree or office through imperial favor without having to compete in the examinations.

The rich had a special advantage in entering the gentry. They could purchase the title of *li-chien-sheng* or *li-kung-sheng* and thus skip the *t'ung-shih*, the examination for admitting *sheng-yüan*. They could then directly participate in the provincial examinations leading to the *chü-jen* degree. . . .

The provincial examinations also gave distinct advantage to the sons and brothers of high officials. Their papers were separated from the rest and marked as "official examination papers," and a separate quota was assigned to them. . . .

When the papers were first checked, the coexaminers almost always recommended

---

[164] Karl A. Wittfogel, in his pamphlet, *New Light on Chinese Society* (New York: Institute of Pacific Relations, 1938), pp. 11-12.

[165] Lattimore, *op. cit.*, p. 49.

[166] Chang, *op. cit.*, pp. 182-187. As clarification for some of the technical terms that follow, it should be pointed out that the examination system comprised three main sets of examinations: (1) those held in the local counties or prefectures, success in which made one a *sheng-yüan*, or "government student" (also known as *hsiu-ts'ai*, "flowering talent"); (2) those held in the provincial capitals, success in which made one a *chü-jen*, "recommended man"; (3) those held in the national capital, success in which made one a *chin-shih*, "presented scholar."

all the "official examination papers" to the chief examiners, while a large proportion of the other papers were eliminated in the first round. . . . With all these
advantages leading sons and brothers of high officials to the degree of *chü-jen*,
the high officials could still exert influence and pressure in the metropolitan examinations. After all, the examiners were their colleagues. . . . In addition, the
bribery and corruption that had always existed in the examinations increased
during the nineteenth century. . . .

However, the greatest inequality of all was in the preparation for the examinations. The poor simply could not afford to spend many years studying for examinations. There was no public education system. Students preparing for *sheng-yüan*
examinations were educated by private tutors or teachers conducting small schools.
. . . Candidates had to pay fees to participate in the examinations. Students had
to pay for each set of examination papers they were to write. . . .

Thus the examination system did not actually afford equal opportunities to all.
Wealth, influence, and family background were powerful factors operating for
the advantage of special groups. Nevertheless, some opportunity did exist for
men without these advantages to rise through their own ability and diligence, and
many men did indeed rise in this way. If there was not equality in the examination
system, there was a general belief in the "spirit of equality," and this belief together with the fact that some social mobility did exist helped to stabilize the
society and maintain the status quo.

It should be emphasized once more that this account describes the examination
system during the nineteenth century, when it was in decline. Nevertheless, some
of the trenchant criticisms—notably that of the financial difficulties faced by the
poor man who wished to educate himself for the examinations—widely apply to
earlier periods as well.

4 Social Mobility: The Gentry

There is no question that the historical records of China are more voluminous
than those of any other long-lived people. Twenty-six major histories exist today
(the earliest compiled about 100 B.C., the latest in the 1920's), which together
provide an unbroken record from earliest times to the founding of the Republic
in 1912. These "dynastic histories," as they are generally known, were in some
cases the work of individuals, in others of imperially appointed boards of
scholars. In toto they are estimated to amount to more than twenty million Chinese characters, which in English translation would be equivalent to over forty-
five million English words.[167]

Of this huge bulk, over 50 per cent consists of biographies of tens of thousands
of individuals: not only officials but also writers, artists, merchants, generals,
rebels, famous women, and many others who, for one reason or another, were
deemed worthy of inclusion. It is hardly surprising that in recent years several
scholars have seen in these materials (supplemented in some instances by collateral sources) the possibility of analyzing statistically the social background
of China's ruling bureaucracy. Among attempts made along these lines we shall
summarize those of Karl A. Wittfogel and Chung-li Chang, both of the Univer-

[167] H. H. Dubs, "The Reliability of Chinese Histories," *Far Eastern Quarterly*, VI (1946),
23-25.

sity of Washington (Seattle), Wolfram Eberhard of the University of California, and E. A. Kracke, Jr., of the University of Chicago.

Most ambitious and sweeping are the conclusions reached by Wittfogel for several of the major dynasties; they are based on data collected over a period of years by members of his well-known "Chinese History Project." These conclusions, presented by him very briefly in a recent publication, are here further summarized by us in the following table (in which "upper-class background" denotes officials who are related to the imperial ruling family, have relatives who are officeholders, or belong to families showing a tradition of government service):[168]

	Percentage of Officials Having	
Dynasty	(a) Upper-Class Background	(b) Commoner Background
Han (206 B.C.-A.D. 220)	92	8
Southern Chin (216-419)[a]	90.5	9.5
T'ang (618-907)[b]	83	less than 10
Sung (960-1279)	85	15
Yuan or Mongol (1234-1368)	85	15
Ming (1368-1644)	77	23

[a] The nomenclature and dating of this period are Wittfogel's own, not generally followed by other historians.
[b] Wittfogel explains that the 7 per cent of the T'ang officialdom not listed here consisted of "barbarians," or outsiders (owing to the fact that the T'ang ruling house itself was, at least in part, of Turkish origin).

It is not inconceivable that these statistics are substantially correct, but the reader unfortunately has no way of judging because Wittfogel, in his summary, provides no indication of how they were reached: the number of biographies used for each dynasty, the basis of their selection, the criteria for distinguishing between upper-class and commoner background, and the like. All such information still remains unpublished in the files of the Chinese History Project.

From this point of view the studies that follow, though far less extensive, are more satisfying. For the Northern Wei dynasty (386-535), Wolfram Eberhard has studied approximately 7,200 persons of all kinds who are mentioned in the history of the dynasty (including 17 per cent or more who, because they lived in areas not ruled by the Northern Wei, should really not be taken into consideration, as well as many others who are recorded for reasons other than their political prominence). Out of this heterogeneous total, nonetheless, Eberhard finds that very nearly 50 per cent came from only 99 powerful families, many of which had records of political activity antedating—sometimes by centuries—the Northern Wei dynasty itself. From this he concludes that "there were very few families originally belonging to the commoners who succeeded in rising into the circle of gentry families." And, again, "The assertion of some authors that there did not exist a leading class in China and that every member of the 'honorable' classes could ascend to the highest ranks of the state by taking the official examinations cannot be maintained for the period in question." [169]

[168] Karl A. Wittfogel, *Oriental Despotism: A Comparative Study of Total Power* (New Haven, Conn.: Yale University Press, 1957), pp. 347-354.
[169] Eberhard, *Conquerors and Rulers*, pp. 116, 120. Eberhard's data are presented in detail in his *Das Toba-Reich Nordchinas: Eine soziologische Untersuchung* (Leiden: Brill, 1949), especially Chap. 3.

For the transitional Five Dynasties period (907-959), Eberhard has arrived at substantially similar conclusions, though on the basis of far fewer data. Of the 109 individuals mentioned in the history as having taken the government examinations during this period, 55 came from well-known gentry families, seven had "personal relations to a gentry family," and only two came from peasant or otherwise socially insignificant families. Unfortunately, however, the family background of no less than 45 of the 109 is not indicated by the history. Yet it is striking that of the 19 individuals known to have *failed* in the examinations, no less than 17 came from these same 45 "unknowns," while only two definitely belonged to gentry families.[170]

For the Sung dynasty, E. A. Kracke has made a valuable study which is based on two documents not actually contained in the dynastic history. These are lists of those individuals (931 in all) who passed the highest government examinations in the years 1148 and 1256. Their particular importance lies in the fact that they give information not only about the successful candidates themselves but also about their brothers, uncles, and paternal forebears (extending back to great-grandfather), with notations as to whether or not these had ever held government office. On the basis of these notations, Kracke is able to reach conclusions significantly different from those of the studies just discussed. Thus of the persons in the 1148 list, he finds that only 43.7 per cent reveal a family tradition of civil service (meaning by this the holding of office either by father, grandfather, or great-grandfather), while for the list of 1256 the percentage is even lower: 42.1 per cent. His conclusion, therefore, is that "unless we find other and more convincing evidence to the contrary, we must accept the conclusion that the examinations of this period regularly served to recruit into the government service a very significant proportion of new blood." [171]

Yet this, as the author himself recognizes, is by no means the end of the story, for in Sung times other avenues existed, besides the examinations themselves, for entering government service. Most important of these was the privilege known as "protection," whereby high-ranking officials could nominate for entrance into the civil service, without examination, a specified number of sons or other relatives (and in some cases even nonrelatives). This privilege (which under later dynasties was virtually abolished) was in Sung times so prevalent that, according to Kracke's estimates, the examinations themselves may have supplied no more than 37 to 50 per cent of the total civil service requirements. Obviously, then, this fact drastically curtails the proportion of new blood brought into the ruling bureaucracy by the examinations alone.[172]

For the Ch'ing or Manchu dynasty (1644-1911), we have already cited Chung-li Chang's study on the nineteenth-century gentry. Among his conclusions is

[170] Wolfram Eberhard, "Remarks on the Bureaucracy in North China during the Tenth Century," *Oriens*, IV (Leiden, 1951), 280-299, especially p. 293.
[171] E. A. Kracke, Jr., "Family vs. Merit in Chinese Civil Service Examinations under the Empire," *Harvard Journal of Asiatic Studies*, X (1947), 103-123. The quotation appears on p. 119.
[172] The percentage of officials recruited through the examinations fluctuated at different periods: around the year 1050 it was roughly 50 per cent, but a century later it had dropped to somewhere between 37 and 44 per cent. For the latter date, see Kracke, "Family vs. Merit," p. 120; for the date of 1050, see his book, *Civil Service in Early Sung China, 960-1067* (Cambridge, Mass.: Harvard University Press, 1953), p. 59.

that at least a third, and probably more, of the persons who acquired examination degrees during this century did so "irregularly," in other words, through purchase rather than actual personal competition in the examinations. (This purchasing of degrees became widespread in the nineteenth century and is one indication of the deterioration of the examination system which then set in.) Another finding, based on 2,146 gentry biographies whose data permit definite conclusions, is that 65 per cent of these belonged to the "established" gentry (comprising men whose fathers or grandfathers possessed gentry status), whereas no less than 35 per cent were "newcomers" (men coming from commoner families). Undoubtedly there is a relationship between this unexpectedly large percentage and the widespread purchase of examination degrees just mentioned.[173]

The assessment of all these and similar statistical studies is complicated by many factors, of which the first is the frequent limitations of the data. We have seen, for example, how Eberhard arrives at conclusions for the Five Dynasties on the basis of 109 cases only, of which no less than 45 lack any indication of family background.

In the second place, it is sometimes possible for different scholars, using different criteria, to arrive at differing conclusions on the same body of material. Among the persons named in the examination lists of 1148 and 1256, for example, we have seen that only 43.7 and 42.1 per cent, respectively, according to Kracke, come from families having a tradition of civil service; the decisive criterion for him is whether or not fathers, grandfathers, or great-grandfathers of the individuals in question held office. Wittfogel, however, broadens the criterion by adding to this category also those men whose brothers or uncles were officeholders; in this way he is able to raise Kracke's percentages to 49.5 and 45.6, respectively.[174]

In the third place, even where scholars agree on the statistical findings, they may disagree on their significance. Eberhard, for example, comments on Kracke's study that whether or not an individual's father or grandfather belonged to the civil service is not in itself necessarily decisive, since even without such paternal background an individual might still belong to the rural (landlord) branch of a gentry family (the city branch of which might include many officeholders). Furthermore, in Eberhard's opinion, the truly vital question is not so much who passed the examinations, but who, in later political life, acquired the really key positions in the hierarchy; most of the latter, according to his theory, came from a small number of gentry families which, however, were politically active over many generations.[175]

In the fourth place, even if social mobility can be shown to have occurred, there is a question, in many cases, whether it is not primarily horizontal in kind (movement into the gentry by persons already possessing recognized wealth and status) rather than vertical (movement from below by actual "nobodies"). Such horizontal mobility seems clearly indicated by the large-scale purchase of exami-

---

[173] Chang, op. cit., pp. 139-140, 214-215.
[174] Wittfogel, Oriental Despotism, p. 352, note k, where, however, he by mistake confuses the two lists, attributing the 43.7 and 49.5 percentages to the 1256 list, and the 42.1 and 45.6 percentages to that of 1148, instead of the other way around.
[175] Eberhard, Das Toba-Reich Nordchinas, p. 366.

nation degrees in the nineteenth century, but it also may have been true of many of the men without apparent official background found in the Sung lists of 1148 and 1256. Such, at least, seems to be Kracke's inference when he writes:[176]

> From what social groups did these latter men come? We know that they included men both from comparatively prosperous and comparatively indigent families, but the relative proportions are not clear. I think we should not be far wrong if we assumed that few acquired the necessary education without one of two advantages: either birth into a family of moderately comfortable economic standing, or into one which, even if poor, had some literary education.

Finally, of course, there is the subjective problem of determining what constitutes "social mobility." If (using some of the figures suggested by Wittfogel) a society, 10 or 15 per cent of whose ruling bureaucracy comes from other social strata, nevertheless remains a "closed" society, by how much must this percentage be raised in order to result in an "open" society? Would an increase to 23 per cent (the figure suggested by Wittfogel for the Ming dynasty) suffice for this purpose, or (as he himself would apparently maintain) would it still be insufficient? And how does the situation reflected by such figures as these compare with that found during the same periods in Europe (where, unfortunately, social mobility can scarcely be measured in the same way)?

Obviously, the answers to these and other complex questions will vary according to different points of view, and for this reason, if for no other, it is unlikely that the controversy over the nature of traditional Chinese society can soon be settled.

5   Social Mobility: The Peasant

There is another way to study the problem of social mobility, and that is from the point of view of the peasant. For premodern times, the available data on peasant life do not permit the kind of statistical analysis which, despite serious limitations, is possible for the gentry. Beginning in the 1920's, however, numerous sociological and economic studies have been made on various segments of contemporary Chinese rural life, from which, despite many variations in detail, it is possible to draw certain over-all conclusions. Although the literature on the subject is enormous, a convenient summary of some of its salient findings is fortunately available in an article by Shu-ching Lee.[177]

On tenancy Dr. Lee writes (citing the classical study of John L. Buck, published in 1937):

> In the wheat region of the North, over three-fourths of the peasants are full owners, while in the rice regions of the Middle and the South less than two fifths are full owners. . . . These regional differences in proportion of tenancy are entirely due to economic causes. In the northern provinces . . . the yield of a farm is too low to be shared by both a landlord and a tenant . . . [whereas] in the rice regions, irrigation makes production of land fairly fruitful. . . . So the high tenancy in the South indicates clearly that the surplus in rice cultivation goes

---

[176] Kracke, Civil Service, p. 69.
[177] Shu-ching Lee, "The Heart of China's Problem, the Land Tenure System," Journal of Farm Economics, XXX (1948), 259-270.

to enrich the urban absentee landowners rather than . . . to improve the level of living of the already poverty-stricken peasants (p. 261).

On tenant-landlord relations:

China has long been overpopulated. Since the peasants who badly need land for cultivation are so numerous and land is difficult to rent, the dealings between the landlord and tenant cannot be on a basis of equal standing. Their relationship resembles the old manor-lord and serf (p. 261).

On land rent:

It is generally agreed among investigators that the rent absorbs approximately fifty percent of the tenant's annual farm produce (p. 262).

On size of land holdings:

Statistical data show that roughly one-third of the peasants hold an area of farm land less than 0.75 acre, one-fifth from 0.75 to 1.50 acres, and one-seventh from 1.50 to 2.10 acres. That is to say that more than 60 percent of the peasants' own less than 2.10 acres (p. 267).

Of particular pertinence to our topic of social mobility is a University of Nanking survey made in 1934-1935 for four different provinces. Its purpose was to determine what proportion of farm laborers, over how long a period of time, could hope to rise in the course of their lives from laborer to tenant farmer, from tenant farmer to part owner, and finally to full owner. Here is Lee's summary of the findings:

The new recruits in farming have to keep on working from boyhood to the age of 31, and then seven out of a hundred of them will have the opportunity of raising their status to that of tenantry. It takes another ten year period of hard work to rise to part ownership [age 41], but the chance is only three out of every two hundred of them, and to shift from part to full ownership, not only seven more years of toil are necessary [age 48], but the possibility drops to one out of every two hundred! In comparison with the tenure situations in the United States, . . . [there] in 1938 almost two out of every five American farmers advanced from tenantship to ownership or from the status of a farm hand to tenantship or ownership (pp. 268-269).

It would obviously be unfair to conclude that conditions typical of the 1920's and '30's have always been equally typical of Chinese history as a whole. Yet many bits of evidence suggest that at a great many periods the life of the peasant has been an extremely hard one. Earliest of these is a text in which an ancient economist, Li K'uei, who lived around 400 B.C., estimates the budget of an average farm family of five persons of his time. Such a family, says Li, cultivates 100 *mou* of land (about 4.75 present English acres), on which it annually produces 150 piculs of grain (about 161 U.S. wheat bushels). Of these 150 piculs, 10 per cent (15 piculs) must be deducted for land taxes, and another 60 per cent (90 piculs) for the family's food, leaving a balance of 45 piculs. This, converted into coinage at the rate of 30 coins per picul, yields a sum of 1,350 coins, of which 1,500 must be expended for clothing and another 300 for sacrifices and other religious observances. The family, as a result, reaches the end of the year with a deficit of 450 coins (15 piculs of grain), and this without allowance being made for illness, deaths, and other possible emergencies. "That is why," Li K'uei concludes sadly, "farmers were constantly in want, and had not the heart to exert themselves in plowing. Instead the price of grain was made excessively dear." [178]

The gravitation of agrarian land into the hands of a small landowning class is a problem that has plagued every major dynasty, and one that none, despite repeated efforts at government intervention, has successfully coped with in the long run. Temporary amelioration and readjustment, nevertheless, have periodically resulted from the bloodletting and political realignments usually accompanying the passage from one dynasty to another. Following the downfall of the final dynasty in 1911, however, this pattern for various reasons did not repeat itself. Indeed, it is entirely possible that, contrary to the sharp rise in living standards brought to the West by the Industrial Revolution, conditions in rural China had by the 1930's deteriorated to the point where they were actually well below what they had been one or two centuries earlier.

Innumerable writers, of course, have cited the failure of Chiang Kai-shek's Kuomintang government to deal effectively with the land problem as a primary—perhaps the primary—cause for its overthrow by the Communists. Shu-ching Lee, for example, writing in 1948, more than a year before the final Communist victory, predicted what was to happen as follows:[179]

> So long as the majority of the peasantry are forced to live in dire privation with no hope of relief, there will always be unrest, dissension and uprising, communist or non-communist. Had the old Kuomintang kept its promises seriously and honestly and carried out in the past twenty years even a moderate land reform . . . , the Communist movement, which is in direct contradiction to China's age-old and deep-rooted familistic ideals, would have lost out in politics. . . . However, if that regime in power continues to act blindly and resorts to military suppression and conquest as the sole means of solution, it will be no surprise that what had happened in France in 1789 and in Russia in 1917 may also happen in China in the near future.

As a summary of the political aspects of Confucianism, the following interpretation—obviously only one of several that might be made—is offered by the present writer:[180]

> Confucian theory . . . has been democratic in the sense that it has consistently emphasized the ideal of government for the people, has tried to counter absolutism by the weight of a morally-educated non-hereditary bureaucracy, and has sanctioned occasional political change as an escape from tyranny. It has been undemocratic, however, in the sense that it has never recognized the need of government by the people as a whole, has always regarded such government as the particular preserve of a small ruling élite, and has sanctioned political change only in terms of shifting personalities, not of basic change in the social and political order.
>
> It is understandable why the Confucianists . . . should . . . refuse to magnify law lest in so doing they cause moral principle to become subordinated to legal form. We may sympathize with their contention that no government is better than the men who operate it, and hence that the moral training of such men counts for far more than any amount of purely legal machinery. The mistake of the

[178] Nancy Lee Swann, *Food and Money in Ancient China* (Princeton, N.J.: Princeton University Press, 1950), pp. 140-142.
[179] Lee, "The Heart of China's Problem," p. 270.
[180] Bodde, "Authority and Law in Ancient China," pp. 54-55.

Confucianists, however, as of all advocates of benevolent paternalism, was their belief that a ruling group, even when free from checks such as would be imposed on it by the presence of influential social groups and forces external to itself, can nevertheless long remain true to its ideals. In Confucian China such checks were weak because, aside from the scholar-official class itself, no such influential social group existed. There was in China nothing comparable to the rise of the urban bourgeoisie of the modern West.

Under these circumstances it is scarcely surprising, therefore, that the noble Confucian ideal of government by merit has, despite many triumphs, too often degenerated into a government by privilege. There is a partial similarity at this point between Confucianism and the ideology of the men who today control the destinies of China. For these men too, like the Confucianists, proclaim the people's welfare to be their highest aim, yet at the same time insist, again like the Confucianists, that the achievement of this aim depends on the leadership of an élite controlling group—in their case the Chinese Communist Party. This is but one of several significant parallels to be found between these two seemingly sharply antithetical ideologies.

Regardless of whether the foregoing interpretation be accepted or not, perhaps it is possible to agree on the following points:

1. No matter how many Chinese, as individuals, may in the course of history have succeeded in climbing into the dominant gentry group, they in so doing never seriously affected its social cohesiveness or ideological configuration. On the contrary, in the very process of entering the gentry they absorbed the values of that class and thus failed to close the gap between it and the population as a whole.

2. While it is obviously unfair to expect to find in traditional China the same values that have been slowly nurtured—often very painfully—in the modern West, one important difference between the two nevertheless deserves mention: the West has been changing for centuries in order to become what it is today, and has done so in good part through forces springing from within itself; China, on the contrary, has, until the past century, changed much less, and then largely in response to forces thrust upon it from the outside. No wonder, then, that the accelerated change to which it has since been subjected should often erupt into revolutionary violence.

3. The Confucian state could function with extraordinary effectiveness so long as it remained—politically, culturally and economically—the self-contained center of "all-under-Heaven." Today, however, as a monolithic entity, it is irrevocably dead, even though its ideas, ideals, and institutions continue, in countless subtle ways, to influence the present scene.

F. SUMMARIES, COMPARISONS, AND CONCLUSIONS

1 The Chinese Philosophy of Organism

At several places we have noted the differences in thinking which in China, as elsewhere, can be expected to occur among different social groups. If, however, we now confine ourselves to purely philosophical levels of Chinese thinking, we find in them, emerging and re-emerging, certain basic complementary patterns which, in their totality, form a homogeneous and consistent world view. In the second volume of his study of Chinese civilization and science, Joseph Needham has identified this world view as constituting, in his words, a *philosophy of organism*. What he means by this term appears in the following two passages:[181]

> Universal harmony comes about not by a celestial fiat of some King of Kings, but by the spontaneous cooperation of all beings in the universe brought about by their following the *internal* necessities of their own natures. . . . In White-head's idiom, the "atoms do not blindly run," as mechanical materialism supposed, nor are all entities specifically directed on their paths by divine intervention, as spiritualistic philosophies have supposed; but rather all entities at all levels behave in accordance with their position in the greater patterns (organisms) of which they are parts (p. 562).

> The development of the concept of precisely formulated abstract laws capable, because of the rationality of an Author of Nature, of being deciphered and re-stated, did not therefore occur [in China]. The Chinese world-view depended upon a totally different line of thought. The harmonious cooperation of all beings arose, not from the orders of a superior authority external to themselves, but from the fact that they were all parts in a hierarchy of wholes forming a cosmic pattern, and what they obeyed were the internal dictates of their own natures. Modern science and the philosophy of organism, with its integrative levels, have come back to this wisdom, fortified by new understanding of cosmic, biological and social evolution. Yet who shall say that the Newtonian phase was not an essential one? (p. 582).

Between this Chinese view and those long current in the West there lies a basic difference: the latter rested on a religious monotheism which saw the universe as initially created, and then organized and operated, by a Divine Being superior to itself; in China, on the other hand, we have seen that the idea of such a creative and controlling deity was absent. Recently, however, among philosophers like Whitehead and physicists like Einstein, an "organismic" view of the universe has been developed, in some respects strikingly similar to ideas expressed long ago in China. In some of the most exciting pages of his book, Dr. Needham advances the theory that this new view may, in part at least, have entered Europe from China via the philosopher Leibniz; for the latter, as is well

---

[181] Needham, *op. cit.*, II, 562, 582.

known, was greatly interested in Chinese thought, which he studied through the writings of the Jesuit missionaries. Here is Needham's challenging conclusion:[182]

> In a word, therefore, I propose for further examination the view that Europe owes to Chinese organic naturalism . . . a deeply important stimulus, if it was no more, in the synthetic efforts which began in the 17th century to overcome the European antimony between theological vitalism and mechanical materialism. The great triumphs of early "modern" natural science were possible on the assumption of a mechanical universe—perhaps this was indispensable for them—but the time was to come when the growth of knowledge necessitated the adoption of a more organic philosophy no less naturalistic than atomic materialism. . . . When it came, a line of philosophical thinkers was found to have prepared the way— from Whitehead back to Engels and Hegel, from Hegel to Leibniz—and then perhaps the inspiration was not European at all. Perhaps the theoretical foundations of the most modern "European" natural science owe more to men such as Chuang Chou [iv-iii cent. B.C.], Chou Tun-i [xi cent. A.D.] and Chu Hsi [xii cent.] than the world has yet realised.

On the Chinese side, we find this basic conception expressed in a network of interrelated ideas in different fields, of which the following is an attempted summary:[183]

> The universe, according to prevailing Chinese philosophical thinking, is a harmoniously functioning organism consisting of an orderly hierarchy of interrelated parts and forces, which, though unequal in their status, are all equally essential for the total process. Change is a marked feature of this process, yet in it there is nothing haphazard or casual, for it follows a fixed pattern of polar oscillation or cyclical return; in either case there is a denial of forward movement. . . .
>
> This cosmic pattern is self-contained and self-operating. It unfolds itself because of its own inner necessity and not because it is ordained by any external volitional power. . . . Human history belongs to the total cosmic process and, therefore, in the eyes of many Chinese, moves according to a similar cyclical pattern. Another . . . view, however, sees antiquity as a golden age and all history since that time as a steady process of human degeneration. . . . [Both views obviously] reject the idea of historical progress, meaning by this a process of progressive improvement.
>
> Though the universe is self-acting and not guided by any volitional power, it is far from being a merely mechanistic universe. Indeed, the very fact that its movements result in life is enough to show that in them must be a principle of goodness. . . . In short, whatever *is* in the universe must be good, simply because it *is*.
>
> The vital link between the nonhuman and human worlds is man's nature, and it necessarily follows from the foregoing that this nature must be equally good for all. If, nevertheless, some men fail to actualize the potentialities of their nature, this is because of their inadequate understanding of how the universe operates. This deficiency, however, can be removed through education and self-cultivation, so that the possibility always exists in theory—though admittedly the chances of its ever being actualized in practice are remote—for all men without exception to achieve sagehood. It thus becomes clear that evil, in Chinese eyes, is not a positive factor in itself. It is . . . the result of man's temporary distortion of the universal harmony.

[182] *Ibid.*, pp. 504-505.
[183] Bodde, "Harmony and Conflict," pp. 67-70.

Human society is, or at least should be, a reflection of this harmony. Hence it too is an ordered hierarchy of unequal components, all of which, however, have their essential function to perform, so that the result is a co-operative human harmony. This means that the ideal society is one in which each individual accepts his own social position without complaint and performs to the best of his ability the obligations attached to that position. Here there seems to be a conflict between this emphasis on social stability and a belief—implied in the doctrine of the potential perfectibility of all men—in social mobility. The two are reconciled, however, by upholding the sanctity of the class structure, yet at the same time recognizing the possibility of social movement for particular individuals. The Chinese examination system was a unique, though imperfect, attempt to give substance to this compromise on the practical level.

War, as the most violent disrupter of social harmony, is, of course, opposed by all save a very few Chinese thinkers. . . .

Cutting across both the human and the natural worlds there are, in Chinese thinking, many antithetical concepts, among . . . [them those of] the Yin and the Yang. . . . In each of these dualisms the Chinese mind commonly shows a preference for one of the two component elements as against the other. At the same time, however, it regards both of them as complementary and necessary partners, interacting to form a higher synthesis, rather than as irreconcilable and eternally warring opposites. Thus here again there is a manifestation of the Chinese tendency to merge unequal components so as to create an organic harmony.

The Sage is the man who to the highest degree succeeds in merging these seeming opposites in himself. . . . He in so doing follows a cycle-like course of withdrawal and return, leading him first from the world of the ordinary to the world of the sublime, but then back once more to the world of ordinary affairs. . . . [Thus] the Sage is both this-worldly and other-worldly, both active and quiescent, so that in him the highest synthesis is achieved.

2 Comparisons between China and the West

Though Western parallels for many of these ideas may be found in various periods and philosophies, they in their totality represent a profoundly different world view:

> Among the points of difference which, on the Western side, seem to be particularly significant, may be cited the belief in a divine act of creation and a divine Power who decrees laws for a universe subordinate and external to himself; antagonistic dualisms of the good-and-evil or light-and-darkness type; original sin, predestination, and personal salvation; individual and class struggle, glorification of war, and belief in historical progress.[184]

What are the reasons for these differences? Are they merely the result of differing stages of development: the fact that the West has had a Renaissance, whereas China, until very recently, remained seemingly medieval? This is apparently the point of view of Fung Yu-lan when he writes:[185]

> China, until very recent times, . . . has remained essentially medieval, with the result that in many respects it has failed to keep pace with the West. . . . We would do well to remember in this connection that what we regard as dif-

---

[184] Bodde, "Harmony and Conflict," pp. 71-72.
[185] Fung, A History of Chinese Philosophy, II, 5.

ferences between eastern and western cultures are in many cases actually only differences between a medieval and a modern culture.

Yet this statement, even if true, explains less than it says, for it tells us nothing concerning *why* China thus remained medieval. Other scholars, however, have developed theories to explain China's distinctive civilization in terms of various economic, technological, geographic and historical phenomena. Unfortunately, they cannot be discussed here for want of space.[186] As a briefer substitute we shall quote the penetrating remarks of the economic historian R. H. Tawney, who, though a self-styled "amateur" in the Chinese field, has nevertheless put his finger on some very basic East-West differences. He begins by throwing out the "medieval" hypothesis: [187]

> The hackneyed reference to the Middle Ages is sadly overworked, and leaves a good deal unsaid. It is misleading, indeed, both in principle and in detail. On the one hand, it implies a comparison of stages of development, as though the Chinese version of civilization, instead of differing in kind from the European, were merely less mature. On the other hand, it ignores the sharp contrasts between them, not only—the most important point—in spirit and quality, but in circumstances and environment. The most obvious of the economic characteristics of mediaeval Europe—to mention no other—was that its population was small, its uncultivated area available for colonisation large, and its sea communications of exceptional excellence. The population of China is large, her unused land resources . . . comparatively small, and the greater part of her territory . . . difficult of access from the sea. It is true, however, that the technique and economic structure of seven-eighths of China recall, though with significant differences, the conditions of life which existed in Europe in the fifteenth century. . . .
>
> In certain of the arts of production, and, still more, of life, she had been a pioneer. But the era of invention, which in the West followed that of natural science, in China preceded it. . . . Methods once crystallised continued unchanged; for, these methods being adequate, and often admirable, change was an evil, which there were few prizes to induce, and no relentless pressure of external circumstances to compel, her to undergo. . . . What elsewhere is forgotten is in China remembered; what elsewhere is a memory is in China a fact. . . .
>
> Such contrasts between the static civilisation of China—as it was formerly called—and the more mobile economy of the West are easily drawn and easily misinterpreted. They are misinterpreted when the differences which they emphasise are assumed to be the expression of permanent characteristics. History, with its record of the movement of leadership from region to region, lends little support to the theory that certain peoples are naturally qualified for success in the economic arts, and others unfitted for it, even were the criteria of such success less ambiguous than they are.
>
> The traditionalism which has sometimes been described as a special mark of Chinese economic life is the characteristic, not of China, but of one phase of civilisation which Europe has shared with her. Rapid economic change as a fact, and continuous economic progress as an ideal, are the notes, not of the history of the West, but of little more than its last four centuries; and the European who is

---

[186] For three well-known theories, see Wittfogel, *Oriental Despotism;* Lattimore, *Inner Asian Frontiers of China;* and Eberhard, *Conquerors and Rulers* (all three of which have been cited earlier). For summary and discussion of the Lattimore and Eberhard theories, see Bodde, "Feudalism in China," pp. 71-82.

[187] R. H. Tawney, *Land and Labour in China* (London: Allen & Unwin, 1932; New York: Harcourt, Brace, 1933), pp. 18-22.

baffled by what appears to him the conservatism of China would be equally bewildered could he meet his own ancestors. During nearly a thousand years, the crafts of the husbandman, the weaver, the carpenter and the smith saw as little alteration in the West as they have seen in the East. In the former, as in the latter, common men looked to the good days of the past, not to the possibilities of the future, . . . [and] accepted the world, with plague, pestilence and famine, as heaven had made it. . . . It is true, however, that for wide ranges of Chinese life, the contrast is valid, though the area to which it applies is year by year contracting. . . .

What is true to-day [1932] is less true than yesterday, and may be false to-morrow. The forces which have caused the economic development of China and the West to flow in different channels are a fascinating theme for historical speculation, but they are one on which a layman is precluded from entering. Naturally, he will remind himself that the question is not merely why the economic life of China has not changed more, but why that of the West has changed so much. Naturally, certain commonplace considerations of geography, history, culture and social institutions will occur to his mind. Naturally, he will recall the position of China, with her vast and relatively homogeneous territory, isolated on the west by mountain barriers, and on the east in contact with civilisations inferior to her own, to whom she gave, and was conscious of giving, more than she received; her patriarchal family system which, far more than the state, has prevented the individual from being crushed by personal misfortune or social disorder, and has weakened the force of economic incentives by making his livelihood the concern and his earnings the property of the family group; the teeming population which that system encouraged and the obstacles to technical improvement offered by the cheapness of human labour; the influence of an educational policy devoted to the encouragement of academic culture and indifferent to the science by which man masters his environment; the philosophy of the Chinese sages, with its scholastic contempt for the merchant and its idealisation of agriculture and the peasant; the small part played in the past by government and law, compared with personal relations, voluntary associations and local custom.

Naturally, he will compare these peculiarities with the characteristics of Europe. He will consider the significance of the long and deeply indented coastline of the latter, . . . which made foreign commerce possible for almost all her regions, and indispensable to some of them. He will recall her possession throughout history of numerous independent centres of economic energy, which fertilised each other by rivalry, imitation and actual migrations. . . . He will ponder the impress stamped on her institutions by Roman law. . . . He will reflect on her early development of a powerful bourgeoisie based on trade and finance, which . . . remade government, law and economic policy, and, when the scientific movement reborn at the Renaissance won its first great triumphs, was alert to turn them to practical account. He will remember the smallness, till recently, of the population of parts of the West in relation to its natural resources, and the consequent stimulus to technical invention.

These are problems, however, which an amateur, unversed in Chinese history and literature, cannot venture to discuss. He must leave the past development of China to the specialist, and confine himself to the task of attempting to note the salient facts in her present economic situation.

3 The Chinese Cultural Tradition Today

Despite the weakening of the Chinese cultural tradition during the past century and a half, the old ideas and attitudes continue to exert their influence, even in the China of Mao Tse-tung. It may surprise readers to realize, for example, that top Communist leaders still find it useful to appeal to Confucian sayings and ideas when exhorting their people to become better citizens or telling them "how to be a good Communist." David S. Nivison of Stanford, who has written an illuminating article on this subject, concludes his analysis by saying, "The Communist need to induce acceptance of authority and uniformity of thought is likely to be a permanent one, and it would seem evident from this study that Confucian ethics, whatever its virtues, can be made to serve this need very persuasively." [188]

Between the traditional Chinese way of life and what happens in China today there is obviously an enormous gap. But there are also certain links which in the final analysis may prove to be equally significant—among them the idea of a trained ruling élite, as well as attitudes toward religion, law, private enterprise, the individual, and the outside world. Of attempts to trace such continuities between Confucian and Marxist China, by far the most able and detailed is that of C. P. Fitzgerald, an English historian who has enjoyed exceptional opportunities for firsthand observation both of pre-Communist and Communist China. Here are a few passages from his provocative book: [189]

> The totalitarian aspect of the Communist regime does not dismay the Chinese people: the Empire was also totalitarian, though the word was not then coined. It was absolute, and so is Communism; it was hierarchic, ruling through a chosen group of specially trained men, the Confucian "Mandarin." So is Communism, ruling by its party, who are brought up on Marx and form a class apart. The Empire had its doctrines, its total explanation of philosophy, politics and economics: the teaching of Confucius. So has Communism, for which Marx as interpreted by Lenin, Stalin and Mao Tse-tung explains all and justifies everything (pp. 117-118).

> The T'ang poets wrote under the shadow of a court as arbitrary and as self-assured as any politbureau. The Sung painters were the high officials of an authoritarian empire constantly preoccupied with the niceties of orthodox doctrine and persecuting the "deviations" of their more original contemporaries. The personal history of the philosopher Chu Hsi, of the Sung period, is a tale of exile, police supervision and persecution, not very different from that of Trotsky. The Court of the Sung "purged," in the most approved modern manner, those of its members whose policy was no longer in favour (pp. 189-190).

> The present generation of recruits, taken into the [Chinese Communist] party in very large numbers . . . are mainly university students, still very young. . . . The new members from these mandarin families are of course ardent Communists. . . . They are also precisely the same group of people who have governed China for the last two thousand years. It is in their blood. They are born to rule, and whether by virtue of Confucius and the Emperor, or Marx and Mao Tse-tung,

[188] David S. Nivison, "Communist Ethics and Chinese Tradition," *Journal of Asian Studies*, XVI (1956), 74. See also the remarks on individualism at the end of Sect. E, 2.
[189] Charles Patrick Fitzgerald, *Revolution in China* (London: Cresset, 1952).

makes very little real difference. Deep rooted . . is the old Chinese conviction that government is an affair for the élite (pp. 193-194).

The Communist world is now the equivalent of the Chinese Confucian world Empire. Those peoples who have received the one orthodox culture, this time Communist, are "civilized" and admitted to the family of nations, those who have not accepted Communism are treated as dangerous and barbarous, each according to the measure of his power and proximity (p. 224).

Underlying the theory and practice of [Chinese Communist] re-education there would seem to be a constant tradition from the past. The bourgeois is a selfish creature who needs to be made to realize his duty to his fellows, but he is redeemable, he can "change his body over," the untranslatable term *fan shen*, which means to undergo the process of conversion. Confucius and his followers . . . also said, "Man is born good, but his nature is corrupted by the evil of the world." . . . What is not found in modern China or in ancient thought is the concept that some special class of citizens has the monopoly of virtue and that all others are for ever damned (p. 267).

Professor Fitzgerald has written a controversial book on a controversial subject. No wonder, then, that it has elicited both praise and attack. Among the more thoughtful of its reviews is that of O. Edmund Clubb, former American foreign service officer who has spent a large part of his life in China:[190]

The author develops two theses of primary importance. First, he points up the critical significance that the position of the intelligentsia bore for the outcome of the revolutionary movement. . . . The second thesis is that the totalitarian regime which has now been imposed on the Chinese people is essentially of the same stuff as the imperial autocracy. . . .

I feel that in his second thesis Professor Fitzgerald has been seduced by an attractive theory, and that he has consequently been led to adopt several positions from which a greater reliance upon the known history of Chinese Communism would have diverted him. In contending in effect that there has been no real change, he disregards the fundamental circumstances that institutional Confucianism was concerned intrinsically with observance of means, that is, procedures and ceremonies, and that the end was by and large maintenance of the status quo; whereas Communism devotes itself to fundamental alteration of the status quo, by any and all means—which have lost all customary and legal sanctity. And the relatively generous local autonomy permitted under the Empire by customary law administered through the village elders has been replaced by a tight "democratic centralism" which is in turn projected into world affairs through "international centralism." Professor Fitzgerald's second thesis is not without suggestive power, and even relevancy; it is inadequate, however, to comprehend the complex phenomenon of Chinese Communism. . . .

By Professor Fitzgerald's own definition, the book was intended to be an essay in interpretation. It admirably fulfills its designed function, and constitutes a useful and stimulating study of confused events in a major field of world interest.

Regardless of how far we are prepared to follow Fitzgerald in his thesis, there is no doubt he has performed one valuable service: his book demonstrates that the past still exists in China. If we today are genuinely interested in understanding China's present, we must make the intellectual effort to understand that past—

---

[190] O. Edmund Clubb, " 'Plus ça change . . .' in China?" *Far Eastern Survey*, XXII (January 28, 1953), 18-19.

in other words, to look at China from within, as a Chinese himself might do. We shall not get far so long as we are content to view the scene in terms of geopolitics, power politics, or any other externalized "political" approach that conveniently ignores several millennia of indigenous forces, institutions, and ideas. This principle indeed seems elementary, yet it is constantly forgotten in our continuing debate on China, even by scholars who should know better.

It further follows that neither from the Chinese nor from any other people can we expect or demand that they will adopt certain values—even those whose superiority seems to us most self-evident—unless within their own cultural past or present-day needs there is compelling reason for so doing. What seems desirable or inevitable to one civilization may seem quite the reverse to another. Long ago, in 1910, a British civil servant long resident in China wrote a book in which—while discoursing on Chinese and Western individualism—he displayed a humbleness and wisdom such as we and the rest of the world could well emulate:[191]

> Even in Europe there are thinkers who have expressed doubts as to whether our Western individualism is not a terribly fragile and unstable foundation on which to build a vast social system; whether there are not already signs of decay in the very bases of our civilisation. The truth of the matter is that there are certain profound social problems which have never yet been solved either by the East or by the West. We are all yet in various experimental stages of social progress. It may be that if Western theories and ideals have soared to greater heights, Eastern theories and ideals have aimed at producing a greater fundamental solidarity; and that, the essential differences being so great, it is inadvisable for either hemisphere to press its ideals too persistently on the other, and dangerous for either to abandon its own ideals too hastily in deference to the other's teaching or example.

Reverting to the present, we leave the reader with a final question which we shall not try to answer ourselves: Are there elements in China's cultural tradition which—not only for China but the world at large—can continue to live today and retain their value? Or is the difference in environment so great that, except as museum pieces, they have lost their relevancy?

[191] R. F. Johnston, op. cit., p. 137.

Bibliographical Note

Space prevents the bringing together here of all the more than one hundred books and articles quoted or mentioned in the main text; on the other hand, to select a few of them only for separate listing would be invidious. Actually, had space permitted, the number of items used could easily have been substantially increased, and one of the most difficult of many problems has been that of selecting certain works at the expense of others almost or equally good. Even so, aside from four or five items, the large literature in languages other than English has been deliberately excluded.

Periodicals published in the United States which are important for scholarly study of China (as well as the Far East generally) include the *Far Eastern Survey* and *Pacific Affairs* (both published by the Institute of Pacific Relations and primarily on the modern scene); the *Journal of Asian Studies* (published by the Association of Asian Studies and known, prior to its sixteenth volume of 1956-1957, as the *Far Eastern Quarterly;* coverage includes all phases of East Asia, both past and present); the *Harvard Journal of Asiatic Studies* (published by the Harvard-Yenching Institute; many articles of high value on premodern China but intended primarily for the specialist); and the *Journal of the American Oriental Society* (mostly on the ancient Near East and South Asia but also some good articles on premodern China).

Bibliographies of value include L. C. Goodrich and H. C. Fenn, *A Syllabus of the History of Chinese Civilization and Culture* (6th ed.; New York: China Society of America, 1958), and the comprehensive current bibliographies published annually in the *Journal of Asian Studies.*

Contemporary China, for understandable political reasons, receives (as of this writing) inadequate and often misleading treatment in American newspapers; the same remarks apply, with only slightly lesser force, to many of the more popular books and articles. For this reason any serious study of Communist China requires the reading of the considerable literature published in England and other foreign countries. English-language periodicals from Communist China itself, such as *People's China* and *China Reconstructs,* are, despite their one-sidedness, often factually useful.

Index

This index includes the names of all authors, editors, or translators mentioned in the text. Works of authors of more than one cited work are listed under authors' names. By consulting these names, therefore, the reader can locate in the main text the initial citations—including full bibliographical information—for all the books and articles (which, in subsequent citations, appear only in abbreviated form or as *op. cit.*).